15 Days of Prayer
With Saint Benedict

Also in the *15 Days of Prayer* collection:

Saint Teresa of Ávila

Pierre Teilhard de Chardin

Saint Bernard

Thomas Merton

Charles de Foucauld

Saint Francis de Sales

Saint Thérèse of Lisieux

Saint Catherine of Siena

Saint Bernadette of Lourdes

15 DAYS OF PRAYER
WITH
Saint Benedict

ANDRÉ GOZIER, O.S.B.

Translated by Victoria Hébert and Denis Sabourin

Published by Liguori Publications
Liguori, Missouri
http://www.liguori.org

This book is a translation of *Prier 15 Jours Avec Saint Benoît*, published by Nouvelle Cité, 1995, Montrouge, France.

Library of Congress Cataloging-in-Publication Data

André Gozier
   [Prier 15 jours avec Saint Benoît. English]
   15 days of prayer with Saint Benedict / André Gozier ; [translated by] Victoria Hébert and Denis Sabourin. — 1st English ed.
       p.   cm.
   Includes bibliographical references.
   ISBN 0-7648-0576-2 (pbk.)
   1. Benedict, Saint, Abbot of Monte Cassino—Prayer-books and devotions—English. I. Title: Fifteen days of prayer with Saint Benedict. II. Title.

BR1720.B45 G6913   2000
269'.6—dc21   99-049651

Scripture quotations are taken from the *New Revised Standard Version Bible*, copyright 1989 by the Division of Christian Education of the National Council of the Churches of Christ in the U.S.A. Used by permission. All rights reserved.

Printed in the United States of America
04 03 02 01 00   5 4 3 2 1
First English Edition 2000

Table of Contents

How to Use This Book

AN OLD CHINESE PROVERB, or at least what I am able to recall of what is supposed to be an old Chinese proverb, goes something like this: "Even a journey of a thousand miles begins with a single step." When you think about it, the truth of the proverb is obvious. It is impossible to begin any project, let alone a journey, without taking the first step. I think it might also be true, although I cannot recall if another Chinese proverb says it, "that the first step is often the hardest." Or, as someone else once observed, "the distance between a thought and the corresponding action needed to implement the idea takes the most energy." I don't know who shared that perception with me but I am certain it was not an old Chinese master!

With this ancient proverbial wisdom, and the not-so-ancient wisdom of an unknown contemporary sage still fresh, we move from proverbs to presumptions. How do these relate to the task before us?

I am presuming that if you are reading this introduction it is because you are contemplating a journey. My presumption is that you are preparing for a spiritual journey and that you have taken at least some of the first steps necessary to prepare for this journey. I also presume, and please excuse me if I am making too many presumptions, that in your preparation for the spiritual journey you have determined that you need a guide.

From deep within the recesses of your deepest self, there was something that called you to consider Saint Benedict as a potential companion. If my presumptions are correct, may I congratulate you on this decision? I think you have made a wise choice, a choice that can be confirmed by yet another source of wisdom, the wisdom that comes from practical experience.

Even an informal poll of experienced travelers will reveal a common opinion; it is very difficult to travel alone. Some might observe that it is even foolish. Still others may be even stronger in their opinion and go so far as to insist that it is necessary to have a guide, especially when you are traveling into uncharted waters and into territory that you have not yet experienced. I am of the personal opinion that a traveling companion is welcome under all circumstances. The thought of traveling alone, to some exciting destination without someone to share the journey with does not capture my imagination or channel my enthusiasm. However, with that being noted, what is simply a matter of preference on the normal journey becomes a matter of necessity when a person embarks on a spiritual journey.

The spiritual journey, which can be the most challenging of all journeys, is experienced best with a guide, a companion, or at the very least, a friend in whom you have placed your trust. This observation is not a preference or an opinion but rather an established spiritual necessity. All of the great saints with whom I am familiar had a spiritual director or a confessor who journeyed with them. Admittedly, at times the saint might well have traveled far beyond the experience of their guide and companion but more often than not they would return to their director and reflect on their experience. Understood in this sense, the director and companion provided a valuable contribution and necessary resource.

When I was learning how to pray (a necessity for anyone who desires to be a full-time and public "religious person"), the community of men that I belong to gave me a great gift. Between my second and third year in college, I was given a one-year sabbatical, with all expenses paid and all of my personal needs met. This period of time was called novitiate. I was officially designated as a novice, a beginner in the spiritual journey, and I was assigned a "master," a person who was willing to lead me. In addition to the master, I was provided with every imaginable book and any other resource that I could possibly need. Even with all that I was provided, I did not learn how to pray because of the books and the unlimited resources, rather it was the master, the companion who was the key to the experience.

One day, after about three months of reading, of quiet and solitude, and of practicing all of the methods and descriptions of prayer that were available to me, the master called. "Put away the books, forget the method, and just listen." We went into a room, became quiet, and tried to recall the presence of God, and then, the master simply prayed out loud and permitted me to listen to his prayer. As he prayed, he revealed his hopes, his dreams, his struggles, his successes, and most of all, his relationship with God. I discovered as I listened that his prayer was deeply intimate but most of all it was self-revealing. As I learned about him, I was led through his life experience to the place where God dwells. At that moment I was able to understand a little bit about what I was supposed to do if I really wanted to pray.

The dynamic of what happened when the master called, invited me to listen, and then revealed his innermost self to me as he communicated with God in prayer, was important. It wasn't so much that the master was trying to reveal to me what needed to be said; he was not inviting me to pray with the same words that he used, but rather that he was trying to bring me to that place within myself where prayer becomes possible. That place, a place of intimacy and of self-awareness, was a necessary stop on the journey and it was a place that I needed to be led to. I could not have easily discovered it on my own.

The purpose of the volume that you hold in your hand is to lead you, over a period of fifteen days or, maybe more realistically, fifteen prayer periods, to a place where prayer is possible. If you already have a regular experience and practice of prayer, perhaps this volume can help lead you to a deeper place, a more intimate relationship with the Lord.

It is important to note that the purpose of this book is not to lead you to a better relationship with Saint Benedict, your spiritual companion. Although your companion will invite you to share some of their deepest and most intimate thoughts, your companion is doing so only to bring you to that place where God dwells. After all, the true measurement of a companion for the journey is that they bring you to the place where you need to be, and then they step back, out of the picture. A guide who brings you to the desired destination and then sticks around is a very unwelcome guest!

Many times I have found myself attracted to a particular idea or method for accomplishing a task, only to discover that what seemed to be inviting and helpful possessed too many details. All of my energy went to the mastery of the details and I soon lost my enthusiasm. In each instance, the book that seemed so promising ended up on my bookshelf, gathering dust. I can assure you, it is not our intention that this book end up in your bookcase, filled with promise, but unable to deliver.

There are three simple rules that need to be followed in order to use this book with a measure of satisfaction.

Place: It is important that you choose a place for reading that provides the necessary atmosphere for reflection and that does not allow for too many distractions. Whatever place you choose needs to be comfortable, have the necessary lighting, and, finally, have a sense of "welcoming" about it. You need to be able to look forward to the experience of the journey. Don't travel steerage if you know you will be more comfortable in first class and if the choice is realistic for you. On the other hand, if first class is a distraction and you feel more comfortable and more yourself in steerage, then it is in steerage that you belong.

My favorite place is an overstuffed and comfortable chair in my bedroom. There is a light over my shoulder, and the chair reclines if I feel a need to recline. Once in a while, I get lucky and the sun comes through my window and bathes the entire room in light. I have other options and other places that are available to me but this is the place that I prefer.

Time: Choose a time during the day when you are most alert and when you are most receptive to reflection, meditation, and prayer. The time that you choose is an essential component. If you are a morning person, for example, you should choose a time that is in the morning. If you are more alert in the afternoon, choose an afternoon time slot; and if evening is your preference, then by all means choose the evening. Try to avoid "peak" periods in your daily routine when you know that you might be disturbed. The time that you choose needs to be your time and needs to work for you.

It is also important that you choose how much time you

will spend with your companion each day. For some it will be possible to set aside enough time in order to read and reflect on all the material that is offered for a given day. For others, it might not be possible to devote one time to the suggested material for the day, so the prayer period may need to be extended for two, three, or even more sessions. It is not important how long it takes you; it is only important that it works for you and that you remain committed to that which is possible.

For myself I have found that fifteen minutes in the early morning, while I am still in my robe and pajamas and before my morning coffee, and even before I prepare myself for the day, is the best time. No one expects to see me or to interact with me because I have not yet "announced" the fact that I am awake or even on the move. However, once someone hears me in the bathroom, then my window of opportunity is gone. It is therefore important to me that I use the time that I have identified when it is available to me.

Freedom: It may seem strange to suggest that freedom is the third necessary ingredient, but I have discovered that it is most important. By freedom I understand a certain "stance toward life," a "permission to be myself and to be gentle and understanding of who I am." I am constantly amazed at how the human person so easily sets himself or herself up for disappointment and perceived failure. We so easily make judgments about ourselves and our actions and our choices, and very often those judgments are negative, and not at all helpful.

For instance, what does it really matter if I have chosen a place and a time, and I have missed both the place and the time for three days in a row? What does it matter if I have chosen, in that twilight time before I am completely awake and still a little sleepy, to roll over and to sleep for fifteen minutes more? Does it mean that I am not serious about the journey, that I really don't want to pray, that I am just fooling myself when I say that my prayer time is important to me? Perhaps, but I prefer to believe that it simply means that I am tired and I just wanted a little more sleep. It doesn't mean anything more than that. However, if I make it mean more than that, then I can become discouraged, frustrated, and put myself into a state where I might more easily give up. "What's the use? I might as well forget all about it."

The same sense of freedom applies to the reading and the praying of this text. If I do not find the introduction to each day helpful, I don't need to read it. If I find the questions for reflection at the end of the appointed day repetitive, then I should choose to close the book and go my own way. Even if I discover that the reflection offered for the day is not the one that I prefer and that the one for the next day seems more inviting, then by all means, go on to the one for the next day.

That's it! If you apply these simple rules to your journey you should receive the maximum benefit and you will soon find yourself at your destination. But be prepared to be surprised. If you have never been on a spiritual journey you should know that the "travel brochures" and the other descriptions that you might have heard are nothing compared to the real thing. There is so much more than you can imagine.

A final prayer of blessing suggests itself:

Lord, catch me off guard today.
Surprise me with some moment of beauty
    or pain
So that at least for the moment
I may be startled into seeing that you are
    here in all your splendor,
Always and everywhere,
Barely hidden,
Beneath,
Beyond,
Within this life I breathe.

Frederick Buechner

REV. THOMAS M. SANTA, CSsR
LIGUORI, MISSOURI
FEAST OF THE PRESENTATION, 1999

A Brief Chronology
of Saint Benedict's Life

BENEDICT WAS COMMONLY known as the patron saint of failures—as he had so many trials in his life. It is said that this was his path to sainthood. Yet, in a certain sense, he bypassed these trials and achieved his goal—the writing of the Rule for the religious community that he founded. He was, if nothing else, a practical man, of decisive character, energetic, reserved in his speech and in the expression of his feelings but extremely ardent. He loved deep thought and was said to have been of a cold demeanor, yet he was positive and loved by his order. He was a counselor for his monks, exacting and benevolent. It is said that he created the Rule by living in the deepest part of himself.

The Rule created by Benedict was condensed from a concrete spiritual experience lived by him and his brothers in their abbey. One of the primary resource materials for the Rule was said to be the Rule of the Master. Although this influence is not certain, other sources that inspired Benedict included Cassian, Saints Augustine, Pachomius, Basil, Jerome, Leo the Great, and the lives of the fathers of the desert. The Rule was created to give life, to bring the person using it to attain a certain experience under the auspices and guidance of the Holy

Spirit. The three pillars of the Benedictine institution are community, the Rule, and the abbot, but liturgical/personal prayer, spiritual reading, and work are the three great values which permit one to live according to the spirit of Saint Benedict.

The majority of what is known about Benedict's life comes from the writings of Pope Gregory the Great (see below). All dates quoted are approximations.

480: Saint Benedict was born to a distinguished and wealthy family in Nursia (today Norcia), Italy.

498: During his studies in Rome, disgusted by the moral squalor of his fellow students, he abandoned his studies in liberal arts and left Rome. He gave up his inheritance, went to Enfide, where he will live until 500, where he will begin his conversion to the monastic life, and where he will become a hermit.

500: He lived in a grotto, which is thought to be near Subiaco, where he remained a hermit until 503.

503: He was visited by a group of monks seeking a spiritual leader; they left together and went to Vicovaro, but the venture failed.

506: There was an attempt on his life by the monks in Vicovaro; they tried to poison his wine because of his different outlook on monastic life which caused them to resent him. When the poisoned wine was brought to him, he blessed it with the Sign of the Cross in his usual manner, after which the vessel shattered before he could drink it. As a result of this event, he left and returned to Subiaco, inaugurated the Abbey of Subiaco, and began the construction of twelve lauras, each with an abbot and twelve monks. These lauras were semiindependent and semieremitical monasteries. All of this occurred after having been sought out by disciples in the wilderness. He remained at Subiaco until 526.

525: Another attempt is made on his life, caused by acute local jealousy.

526: He transported his group of monks to Monte Cassino, in the province of Campagna (which is midway between Rome and Naples), where he inaugurated the Abbey of Monte Cassino. It is considered to be the birthplace of the Benedictine order.

530 (approx.):

The Rule of Benedict is written, inspired by the events of 506. It was written in *ingua vulgaris* (low Latin). His own personality is mirrored in his description of what kind of man an abbot should be: wise, discreet, flexible, learned in the law of God, but also a spiritual father to his community. Benedict was not a priest, nor did he intend to found a religious order. His main achievement was to write the Rule.

547: Benedict died in Monte Cassino near the altar where he received the Blessed Sacrament, while his monks held up his arms in prayer.

577: Monte Cassino is destroyed by the Lombards.

593–594:

Pope Gregory the Great writes *The Dialogues* (books 1–4), which are interviews by Peter the Deacon about Saint Benedict's life work and his thoughts concerning monastic life.

8th Century:

According to what was written at the time, March 21 has become recognized as a day of veneration dedicated to Benedict.

896: The original Rule written by Saint Benedict himself was destroyed. It was burnt when the reconstructed Monte Cassino was again burned down.

In modern times, Saint Benedict was proclaimed patron saint of Europe in 1964 by Pope Paul VI. In 1969, the Roman calendar permanently moved his feast day to July 11 so as not to observe it during Lent.

A Few Notes About Saint Benedict

15 Days of Prayer With Saint Benedict is supported by two fundamental texts: Saint Benedict's Rule (or the Monk's Rule) and the Life of Saint Benedict, an extract drawn from the book, *The Dialogues*, by Saint Gregory the Great. It is the only hagiography that exists for the life of the patriarch of monks.

The Rule of Benedict is believed to have been drafted between 530 and 540 and was constantly revised and improved as a function of Saint Benedict's experience. We must, however, note a cultural gap with our present day. We must "crack the shell in order to get to the fruit"! The fruit is wisdom, extracted from these reflections to help us lead our lives, which may be as useful for the coming of the millennium as it has been in the past.

In this era of interreligious and intermonastic dialogue, we have occasionally made comparisons and noted similarities with the Asian monasticisms (Hinduism, Buddhism) and with Sufism. We could have added even more.

Just as in Zen monasteries, the subject is led—by means other than the paths set out by Saint Benedict—to discover the truth of his existence. But this descent towards nothingness is the starting point of an elevation which, in Christianity, leads to divinization. As Scripture says: "Those who humble themselves will be exalted" (Lk 14:11).

Abbreviations Used
in This Book

RM   The Master's Rule.

RB   Saint Benedict's Rule. The number that follows refers
      to the chapter.

D   *The Dialogues* written by Saint Gregory the Great or
      the *Life of Saint Benedict* from the translation done by
      the Benedictines of Paris. Ed. De La Source, 1952.

Introduction

"Benedict dwelled with himself." (D, 3)

DWELLING WITH OURSELVES

Saint Gregory the Great tells us in Book 2 of *The Dialogues*—the life of the blessed Father, Saint Benedict—about types of "Benedictine fioretti," or miracles, which played an important role after the failure of the reform of Vicovaro: "Benedict returned to his beloved solitude and, alone, under the gaze of the Supreme Witness, he dwelled with himself."

He "dwelled with himself" is an admirable formula which, fortunately for us, Gregory's interviewer—Peter the Deacon—misunderstood. Gregory then began to explain, supported by the parable in Luke 15:11–32.

> We will say that this prodigal son was with himself and went into a far region, eating up a part of his inheritance, reduced to herding pigs. What do the Scriptures say? Having regained his senses, he said, "I will come to my Father." If he had lived with himself, from where will he have come back?

Assuredly, the prodigal child did not dwell within himself.

He was lying to himself. In order to dwell within oneself, we must begin by returning to ourselves. That is the first step, the first level of significance to Gregory's formula, but there are others. We must insist here on solitude, which plays an important role in this return.

Here is the second level as indicated a little further on in Gregory's writings. He tells us that:

> Benedict lived with himself, there, he kept himself inside of barriers that he imposed on the processes of his thoughts.

It was there where the battle against thoughts, which were so important to the Desert Fathers, took place, for Benedict inherited it all from oriental monasticism. In effect, this battle is very dear to all monastic traditions, for by attending to our thoughts, we also attend to daily activities by detaching ourselves from them. We learn, through humility, that the origin of thought is deeper than we think (see RB, 7), by attributing all that is good within us to God, but also by recognizing that the evil in oneself is attributable only to oneself (see RB, 4). In the Hindu context, one constantly asks oneself the question: who am I? Then, we will be established in truth.

However, to dwell with oneself is the first step, to come back to oneself by leaving the area of dissimilarity (that is to say, sin), for we are created in the image and likeness of God (Gen 1:36).

Then to the second step: To attend to our thoughts and actions. This great step means is to "live under the watchful eye of the Supreme Witness," in the presence of God. Then, little by little, we establish ourselves in the area of resemblance to God.

But this area of resemblance will bring us to perceive a

third step—or level—of significance. It is necessary here to pass from an exterior God to an interior God, from a divine presence that is exterior to ourselves to a divine presence that is interior, to a perception of self (with a lowercase letter) invested and inhabited by the Self (with an uppercase letter), that is, God. The soul is alone with God but, in him, it finds the world. That is the meaning of Benedict's great vision which will be the subject of our last chapter.

There, Peter the Deacon understands nothing at all and Gregory explains to him:

> Peter, remember what I say to you: In as much as the contemplative has caught a glimpse of the light of God, all that is created becomes too narrow for him; for the light of contemplation broadens the capacity of the soul and thus his spirit becomes dilated, and he receives an interior light which shows him how restricted everything is that is not God.

All spiritual life is a progression towards this awakening to the interior light and its coming is as certain as the dawn, to cite an expression from the prophet Hosea (6:3).

It is necessary to let God awaken in the depth of the soul, to let it be God in the soul, to let it take his happiness in the soul. To dwell with the self (with a lowercase letter) becomes dwelling with the Self (with an uppercase letter), for "anyone united to the Lord becomes one spirit with him," according to Saint Paul's formula (1 Cor 6:17). That is the area of union.

Perhaps we could risk making a comparison here with Islam. The greatest Sufis and Hallaj had particularly understood the "tawhid" as a unification of self in the self and a unification of self in God, that which evokes the return of the soul to its source of being. Didn't Benedict speak of "returning to God"? Or again perhaps we could risk pointing out another similarity with the hesychia, which can be translated to include many inseparable words: solitude, tranquility of heart, rest, detachment, retreat into oneself maintained by a vigilance to unite the personal depth where God is. Hesychia is very dear to Eastern Christian monasticism, particularly at Mount Athos.

INTERIORIZATION

Monasticism, at its very foundation, is a movement of interiorization. Whether it is Hindu, Buddhist, or Christian, it can be defined in this way. It is clear that solitude holds a primordial and essential place. By interiority, we mean the movement by which the spirit deepens itself in the search for its foundation. In Christianity, more precisely, it is an effort of the spirit to go beyond itself towards God with a vision of finding God in itself, beyond itself, "through the path that the Gospel has cleared for us" (RB, Prologue), lived integrally.

To get back to his principle, for Saint Benedict, it meant a return to God. This return is conditioned by a search for God, and the goal of such a search is unification.

In effect, the monks are called thus (according to the writings of Pseudo Dionysius the Areopagite—around the year 500 A.D.—in the book *The Ecclesiastical Hierarchy*, chapter 6) "because they exercise the religion in a pure manner, that is to say, service to God and because their life, far from being divided, remains perfectly one, because they unify themselves by holy withdrawal which excludes all distractions in order to tend towards the unity of a conduct that conforms to God and towards the perfection of divine love."

It is, then, to dig deeper into what is within in order to find the source, the Self.

Monasticism flourished in different ways in the East and in the West, under the eremitical form as exampled by Saint Anthony the Great, c. 251–356), under the cenobitic form (living together under a rule, under an abbot, more exacting than the life in the ashrams and, in principle, until death), with Saint Basil (c. 329–379), and Saint Pachomius (c. 287–347). Saint Benedict greatly admired the hermits, but he legislated only for the cenobites, "the strongest and best type of monks" (see RB, 1) and considered Saint Basil to be "our Father" (RB, 73).

Cenobitism was a vehicle to free the hermits from all matters material and temporal, from their own wills, that is, things that were self-oriented in order to train them under the direction of an elder—the abbot—who had the experience of God.

Cenobitism is constituted by the total spiritual relationship of each of its members to a man who represents Christ—an abbot or a superior. From this relationship flows the relationships of the brothers amongst themselves.

It is in the extension of eremitism in this sense that it forms the framework to help the monks to "truly seek God" (RB, 58). It is an organization on a communal scale of the paternal spirituality of the Desert Fathers, for the mission of the abbot flows from a solitary relationship with God and it tends to lead the soul to this authentic meeting in an authentic solitude.

The word "monk" comes from the Greek word "monos," which means "oriented exclusively towards a single end, chaste, not shared." The meaning has evolved to signify: one, sole, solitary, finally unique, the one who realized this unity, the one who tends to this unity.

The central theme of this fifteen-day retreat with Saint Benedict is to "truly seek God" (RB, 58). But how do we "truly seek God"? That is what we will explain by beginning with stripping the soul in order to finish by a rediscovery of the world, but this time, in God through contemplation.

15 Days of Prayer
With Saint Benedict

DAY ONE

Listen

FOCUS POINT

There are distractions that enter our lives on a regular basis. If we pay too much attention to these distractions, we are unable to truly listen, unable to give God our full attention. And it is only when we listen to God with our whole heart, without distraction, that we are most aware of God's will for our lives, and most aware of the love shared between creature and Creator. Let us pray that the distractions which enter our lives may be short-lived, and that these distractions will succumb to a settled heart ready to listen for God's voice.

Listen, my son, and with your heart hear the principles of your Master. Readily accept and faithfully follow the advice of a loving Father, so that through the labor of obedience you may return to Him from whom you have withdrawn through the influence of disobedience.

To you, therefore, my words are now addressed, whoever you are, who, renouncing your own will, takes up the most powerful and brilliant armor of obedience in order to fight for the Lord Christ, our true King.

First of all, when beginning any good work, beg of Him with most earnest prayer to perfect it, so that He who is now pleased to number us among his children may not at any time be made sorrowful by our evil actions. For we ought at all times so to serve Him using the gifts He has entrusted to us, that He may neither, as an angry Father, at any time disinherit his children, nor, as a dreaded Lord, offended by our evil deeds, deliver us to everlasting punishment for refusing to follow Him to glory.

Now let us arise, since Scripture stirs us up, saying: "It is now the hour for us to rise from sleep" (Rom 13:11). Now let us open our eyes to the divine light and attentively hear the Divine voice, calling and exhorting us daily, "Today if you hear his voice, do not harden your hearts" (Ps 95:8). And again, "He who has an ear, let him hear what the Spirit says to the Churches" (Mt 11:15, Rev 2:7). And what does He say: "Come O children, listen to me; I will teach you the fear of the Lord" (Ps 34:11), and "Walk while you have the light, that darkness may not overtake you" (Jn 12:35).

And the Lord, seeking his own laborer in the multitude of the people to whom He addresses the previous admonitions, says again: "Who is the man that will have life, and desires to see good days?" (Ps 34:12). And if, hearing this, you answer "I am he," God says to you: "If you will have true and everlasting life, keep your tongue from evil and your lips from words of deceit. Forsake evil and do good; seek after peace and pursue it. And when you have done these things, my eyes will be upon you and my ears shall be open to your prayers. And before you shall call upon me, I will say, Lo, here I am."

What can be more appealing, dear brothers, than the voice of the Lord's invitation? See how He shows us the way of life in His benevolence (RB, Prologue).

SILENCE

In the prologue to his Rule, Saint Benedict promises that the Lord himself will show us "the road of Life," that is to say, the Gospel. We are advised by Benedict to walk on this path, or even run there. Also, says the prologue, if, today, you hear his voice, do not harden your hearts to his message.

To walk this path, it is necessary only to return to the One who "had distanced you from the laziness of disobedience," says Benedict's prologue. In fact, all of Saint Benedict's Rule is directed at this goal. It synthesizes all of his experiences. Written at Monte Cassino, he constantly corrected, modified, and improved it. It is filled with biblical citations, because the Rule is there to put the Word of God into action, not to replace it. For the monk, what is contained in the Rule forms his evangelical life. It does not speak of an "exterior Jesus," of the one who went from place to place with his disciples to proclaim the Good News. Saint Benedict's Christ is the "interior Christ," the one who lived within the abbey, the visitors, the brothers, the one who calls in the depth of the heart.

The Rule, which is referred to as "the completed lesson, the definition of the monastic ideal" because it brings back the entire past tradition, opens with a warm request made by Saint Benedict to listen. To listen to whom? To God, for it is he who is speaking. He speaks in different ways, but in a very special way through the Bible. In order to be able to hear, we must begin by being silent. In order to return to God, we must be quiet.

One cannot "live with himself" if there is a distraction. Silence is the master of all masters, because it teaches without words. It is in the silence of the cloisters of Monte Cassino that a way of life was born, that is to say, a series of reflections regarding the way life should be led—in short, the Rule of Benedict. It is through silence that we can again find our true nature, the true meaning of our existence, from which we learn to know ourselves and measure our wealth and poverty, where we penetrate the center of our soul. "Homo Benedictus" is a person who has returned to himself, and who blazes the way to the discovery of our own souls.

In order to come back to one's self, we must accept ourselves with our limitations, accept others, accept what we are.

It is in silence that we will find righteous thoughts again. In order to have a righteous thought, we must have a heart that seeks to be purified. If the thoughts are righteous, the words will be righteous, that is to say, for Saint Benedict, our "language" and actions will also be righteous, that is, "the hands and the feet." All of it leads us to righteous behavior, that is, "discretio" or discernment. A comparison with Buddhism would be simple to make.

Silence is the subject of Chapter 6 of the Rule. Above all, we recall Saint Benedict's expression: "through the love of silence." This practice of silence is not complete muteness, but a restriction in speech. If a monk establishes a certain solitude for himself, it is done so that he can hear God better. "At all times, he must study in silence" (RB, 42).

WORDS

"Let us open our eyes to the Divine light and attentively hear the Divine voice, calling and exhorting us daily," writes Benedict in his prologue. What is this "Divine light" if it is not the one that the Nicene Creed (325 A.D.) proclaims as the "light of lights," Christ who deifies us? Whose voice is it that cries out to us every day, if it is not the voice of Christ which knocks at the door of our hearts: "Listen! I am standing at the door knocking; if you hear my voice and open the door, I will come in to you and eat with you, and you with me" (Rev 3:20)? What can be sweeter, says Benedict, more pleasing, my beloved brothers, than hearing the voice of the Lord's invitation? (RB, Prologue).

This established silence, and it is always something to be established and won back in order to be able to listen, will permit us to hear the Master's words and to tune the ear of our heart to them, because we must descend to a level of our being that is not superficial in order to be able to truly listen.

Silence puts us into a state to receive the teaching and, once there, to receive the promise of happy days. Who wouldn't open their ears to that? There, where the voice of the Lord is gentle and where, in his goodness, he shows us the road to eternal, spiritual life. Who wouldn't want to follow that road?

The voice is the totality of all sounds emitted which transmit the word. To speak is to manifest, to express our thoughts, to reveal what is hidden. Therefore, the voice transmits the word. Better yet, when the voice expresses an idea, it becomes the word. Better still, when the voice and the word unite, then the word manifests itself, the mental voice is uttered.

The voice is then at the service of the word. The word is the Word of God, in God, of the Son of God, his perfect expression. But for this Word to reach us, it became flesh, it became the Word which was uttered in the phenomenon of the Incarnation, in history.

Christ appeared only once in a visible way and now, every day, this same Word-made-flesh comes to us under the cover of a human voice, said Saint Benedict. To be able to discern the Voice from all that happens to us, is to hear the voice of the Word-made-flesh speaking to us; when that event—that is to say, when the voice and the Word-made-flesh unite and reach us—it expresses the divine will for us.

We have to learn to listen to these events which occur both in the liturgy and outside of it as if they are God's words. It is thus that we will return to God, make our lives become holy, by God intervening in our lives, as he intervened for Israel. But Israel didn't listen. That is why we have to say, as does the little Samuel: "Speak, for your servant is listening" (1 Sam 3:10).

These "events" are given to us in order to help us serve Him, but they are, above all, building materials to help us construct our response to the Word in order to return to God. And, with time and spiritual progress, we will perceive—and marvel at—that his all-powerful grace (for it frees our freedom) sustains, gives power to, constructs, guides, steers, and better fulfills the response that is our life. Grace is not only the architect, but also the mason of our "yes" to the event.

And then, in the knitted fiber of our existence, which is chaotic at times, God not only picks up single stitches, but entire rows that have been slipped off, for he knows "...that all things work together for good for those who love God" (Rom 8:28), even negative things.

After having brought the disciple back to his heart, to his center, Benedict mentions the mysterious guest that operates in him. Then he could say, with the prophet: "Praise the Lord"

(Ps 113:1), and with Saint Paul: "But by the grace of God I am what I am..." (1 Cor 15:10).

REFLECTION QUESTIONS

Do I attempt to listen for God's voice with my whole heart, with my full attention? Do I allow distractions to disrupt my spiritual life? Might the discipline of some prayer practice (for example, twenty minutes of centering prayer each evening) hone my listening into better form and better develop my communication in prayer to God?

Is my spiritual life a fearless walk toward God—an ascension based on simplicity and docility? Do I see disobedience as the real root of sin? Do I acknowledge with my whole mind and hear that it is sin which upsets the very balance of my being?

DAY TWO

Look for God

―――

FOCUS POINT

Looking for God, like waking up in the morning, involves a certain amount of taking away and putting on. When we awake each morning, so many of us wipe the "Sandman's Dust" from our eyes before putting on our glasses, so that we can face the day with clear sight. Likewise, and in a spiritual fashion, we wipe away those actions in our lives that do not bring us closer to God, while adding to our daily repertoire those activities which unite us in love to God and neighbor.

―――

To him who newly comes to conversion let not an easy entrance be granted, but as the apostle says: "Test the spirits to see if they are of God" (1 Jn 4:1). If therefore he who has come perseveres in knocking, and after four or five days seems patiently to endure the wrongs done to him and the difficulty made about his entrance, and he persists in his petition, let entrance be granted to him and let him be lodged in the guesthouse for a few days.

Afterward let him live in the cell of the novices where he shall meditate, eat, and sleep. Let there be assigned to him a senior who is skilled in winning souls, who may watch him with the utmost care and consider carefully whether he truly seeks God, is zealous for the works of God, for obedience and for humiliations. Let there be set before him all the difficult and rugged ways by which we walk toward God (RB, 58).

THE INSTRUMENTS OF GOOD WORKS

Established in silence in order to better hear the Word of God which comes to us through the liturgy, Bible reading, the abbey, the brothers, and our heart, these good works "create the event," in as much as they echo within us. Saint Benedict, a practical man, has then put into the hands of his disciple a catalogue "of instruments for good works" or of perfection, which, in general, are borrowed, more or less literally, from the holy Scriptures. These tools of perfection must be diligently manipulated in the workshop, which is the cloister of the monastery. We will also take note of his concern for the weak.

Here, then, is the list "of the instruments of the spiritual art" (or good works). Benedict says of his list,

Behold, these are the tools of the spiritual craft, which, if we use them day and night, and duly give them back on the day of Judgment, the Lord will give us the reward that he promised: "…what no eye has seen, nor ear heard, nor the human heart conceived, what God has prepared for those who love him" (1 Cor 2:9). And the workshop where we are to work diligently at all these things is the cloister of the monastery and the stability of the community.

Benedict lists seventy-two of these instruments in Chapter 4 of his Rule. Here they are.

1. In the first place, to love the Lord God with all our heart, soul, and strength.
2. To love one's neighbor as oneself.
3. Not to kill.
4. Not to commit adultery.
5. Not to steal.
6. Not to covet.
7. Not to bear false witness.
8. To respect all men (1 Peter 2:17).
9. Not to do to another what one would not have done to oneself.
10. To deny oneself in order to follow Christ.
11. To chastise the body.
12. Not to love pleasure.
13. To love fasting.
14. To comfort the poor.
15. To clothe the naked.
16. To visit the sick.
17. To bury the dead.

18. To aid those in trouble.
19. To comfort the sad.
20. To reject worldliness.
21. To love Christ above all else.
22. Not to become angry.
23. Not to show temper.
24. Not to keep deceit in one's heart.
25. Not to make a false peace.
26. Not to forsake charity.
27. Not to swear, for fear of committing perjury.
28. To speak the truth with heart and lips.
29. Not to return an evil for an evil.
30. Not to injure anyone, but to accept patiently any injury to oneself.
31. To love one's enemies.
32. Not to insult those who insult one, but to praise them.
33. To suffer persecution for the sake of justice.
34. Not to be proud.
35. Not to drink to excess.
36. Not to be a glutton.
37. Not to love sleep.
38. Not to be slothful.
39. Not to murmur.
40. Not to slander.
41. To put one's trust in God.
42. To attribute to God the good one sees in oneself.
43. To recognize that the evil in oneself is attributable only to oneself.
44. To fear Judgment Day.
45. To fear hell.
46. To desire eternal life with all one's spirit.
47. To see death before one daily.

48. To monitor one's actions ceaselessly.
49. To know for certain that God sees all everywhere.
50. To dash one's evil thoughts against Christ immediately, and to reveal them to one's spiritual advisor.
51. Not to speak evil or wicked speech.
52. Not to speak much.
53. Not to speak idly nor so as to cause mirth.
54. Not to love boisterous laughter.
55. To enjoy holy reading.
56. To often partake of prayer.
57. To confess past sins to God daily in humble prayer and to avoid these sins in future.
58. Not to succumb to the desires of the flesh.
59. To despise one's own will.
60. To obey the abbot's commands in all things, even if he strays from his own path, mindful of the Lord's command: "What they say, do, but what they do, do not perform" (Mt 23:3).
61. Not to desire to be called holy before the fact, but to be holy first, then called so with truth.
62. To fulfill God's commandments in one's activities.
63. To love chastity.
64. To hate no one.
65. Not to be jealous or envious.
66. To hate strife.
67. To evidence no arrogance.
68. To honor the elderly.
69. To love the young.
70. To pray for one's enemies for the love of Christ.
71. To make peace with an adversary before sundown.
72. Never to despair of God's mercy.

The last two instruments represent the final summing up of Saint Benedict's whole teaching on forgiveness and hope. Two aspects of the virtue of charity are implied in these two injunctions: Nothing should be allowed to mar the harmony of the community or the balance of the individual soul, and even if one has failed to observe all the requirements of the list, God's mercy is still there to be taken advantage of.

IS A FAITH THAT NEVER ACTS A SINCERE FAITH?

We will note Saint Benedict's concrete side. Faith manifests itself and develops through action. We could easily compare this list with certain catalogues we find in Buddhist monasticism. Knowing the difficulties that Catholics encounter in order to make their confession, we could suggest that they consult Chapter 4 of the Rule as a means of examining one's conscience in their search for God.

REFLECTION QUESTIONS

As I read the seventy-two "instruments of good works," do I see any new ways to add and subtract thoughts and actions from my everyday life for the benefit of my spiritual life? Does God's love for me and all creation become clearer when I apply these instruments to my daily life? Which of the seventy-two instruments serve as my biggest challenge? Might a prayer for God's grace in addressing this challenge benefit my spiritual life?

Do I exercise the underlying virtue of these "good works": that of charity? Have I avoided clothing the naked, visiting the sick, burying the dead, and consoling the sorrowful as merely

antiquated notions? Do I practice some measure of self-renun-
ciation, curbing my speech, forgoing anger or revenge, and
not to seek after luxuries that soften resistance to sin.

DAY THREE

Accompaniment

FOCUS POINT

An invaluable tool in the spiritual life is a spiritual guide or director. As an objective observer and insightful "sounding board," the spiritual director can identify those aspects of the directee's life to which one may be blind and neglectful to the detriment of one's relationship with God. The directee's determination to open one's heart to the fullest, and experience the insights of the director, is critical to spiritual growth.

The fifth step of humility is achieved when a monk, by humble confession, discloses to his abbot all the evil thoughts in his heart and evil acts he has carried out (RB, 7).

THE ABBOT

For Benedict, what is important in the monastic tradition is an opening of conscience. When one wants to explore unknown territory, one takes a guide. That is why the person who seeks interiority turns to someone who can help him, the spiritual Father. He is a Father because he gives life; he is spiritual because it is the life of the Holy Spirit that he gives.

This paternity is not a vague metaphor because the guide leads him into a new world. It engenders the divine life. It is a true transmission of life, a new birth (Jn 3:1–2). The Father is the primary source of life. Cenobitism (monastic life) consists of a meeting between a man and another man who represents Christ and takes his place. The abbot unites his spiritual sons who are drawn, one by one, by the radiance of his personality and the fullness of life that he exhibits. We must recognize that this guide, this spiritual master, is not always easy to find. In order to totally give himself to God, the disciple hands his temporal care and the management of his existence over to his abbot. The cenobitic society is an elaboration of the eremitical experience. Saint Benedict did nothing more than to propose to the monk, within the framework of the ideal community life of contemplative solitude, a life of complete solitude. It is not a gathering as such around a holy monk that is really sought, but it is a gathering around the spiritual master. It is similar to the monasticism of India where the one who is the center of the ashram is the "darsana" or guru. In times past, one went to consult the Father in the desert, today, one stays close to him in order to gain the benefit of his teachings for one's entire life.

He teaches through his actions and his words. This search for God, to which he summons his disciple, should take up his entire existence. That is why he tells him what he must do, because work plays a very great role in Benedictine as well as in Zen monasteries. In Chapter 48, Saint Benedict stated that idleness is an enemy of the soul. "Pray and work" was the motto given to the Benedictine order. It is for this reason that the Father gave his disciple instructions about what occupations he was to do: craftsman, farmer, teacher, social worker, scientist, religious. No matter what he did, he was to work, he had duties and functions (see RB, 48, 50, 57, 62, 65, 66, 67).

The spiritual master understood others to the depth of his own being. He must draw and illuminate them by taking them back to their interior master—their soul. The teachings within corroborated the teachings that were externally received.

He must awaken, elicit, and develop their spiritual desire. The abbot is assisted by "the elders" who act like lamps that enlighten and shine. They help the abbot with the healing which enables the disciple to see, as he has been blind from birth (see Jn 9:1–40), but they disappear before the light. They say what they have seen and heard from the interior master in the silence of the heart.

After having been trained, the disciple finds what he has within himself, but a mediation is necessary—words spoken by a spiritual master—which remind him of his rank and place: "The words that I have spoken to you are spirit and life" (Jn 6:63). The Scriptures which are explained and lived by the abbot are a sign; they send the chosen ones back to the interior Master.

THE COMMUNITY

The community is engendered by the abbot, but the community is not the goal, people are not there to serve the community. The people and the community are at God's service, which is not the same thing. Therefore, the community personalizes the being of each person because each person receives from some and gives to others, each of them completing themselves in this way. But the community makes demands, calls for and exacts the sacrifice of the individual for the good of others. By doing this, the monk identifies himself with the person of Christ. Sanctification by the total being brings with it more crosses than joys for some, but one of the major aspects of Benedictine cenobitism is the interpersonal relationships created in the search for God. To neglect this would be to deny the Benedictine institution and erase the second commandment. Christ came to save human relationships, as much as he could, so that they should be participated in through love, and unite divine people in their midst. Also, the personality of each person grows since it unites its own values with those of the community and, in return, the fullness of community life elevates and enriches the personalities to the extent that the community is at the forefront in the thoughts and efforts of its individuals.

Lay people could benefit from being accompanied spiritually by the abbot or, more often, by the spiritual Fathers designated by him to assist him in this function. But neither monk nor layperson will receive anything from the Father unless he opens his conscience as wide as possible and is disposed to listening.

We note that the guru in the ashrams of India, at least in the nondualist traditions, is considered by his followers in such a way that the "I" of the master in his ultimate level is the "He" (Brahman) and that he has "passed" to the Realization.

But the abbot is aware of the fragility of each person and oversees what happens with a sense of moderation, because there are those who are frail, and that awareness applies to ascetic efforts as well as for the division of labor. As Benedict states in Chapter 48 of the Rule:

On Sunday, they [the monks] are to devote themselves to reading, with the exception of those who are assigned to various duties. But if there is one who is so negligent and slothful as to be unwilling or unable to meditate or read, let some work be given him to do so that he may not be idle. As for those brothers who are sickly or weak, let such a work or craft be assigned to them that they may be neither idle nor oppressed by the burden of their labor, so as to quit the monastery. The abbot must take their weakness into consideration.

It is the opening of our heart to God, to the abbot, that is the last step given to us in order to reach the truth within ourselves, to truly become ourselves.

REFLECTION QUESTIONS

In the midst of God, as well as in the presence of our spiritual director, an open heart is necessary for honest and beneficial communication. This is a humble heart without pretense. To what degree am I humble when I encounter God? To what degree am I open and honest—holding nothing back—with my spiritual director? What are those obstacles preventing me from becoming myself in the face of God and in the course of spiritual direction? Pride? Fear? Am I determined to pray for God's grace in my effort to overcome these obstacles?

If my heart is truly open, are my ears open as well? Do I hear what my director has said to me in a spirit that is not self-deceptive and one that is based on a sincere wish for forgiveness and advice?

DAY FOUR

Obedience

FOCUS POINT

In the Benedictine monastery, the abbot represents Christ, and the monks of the monastery are obedient to their abbot because he represents Christ and it is Christ's will the monks wish to serve. In our daily lives we, too, try to mold our will to that of Christ, since it is he who knows what is best for us, what will make us truly happy. We shape our will to Christ's by following the commandments he followed, by learning from our great Teacher's scriptural words, and by regular prayer to our Lord.

The first degree of humility is obedience without delay. This obedience is characteristic of those who hold nothing dearer than Christ, and who because of the holy service which they

have taken upon themselves, or on account of the fear of hell,
or for the glory of eternal life, as soon as anything has been
commanded by their superior, as though it were commanded
by God himself, cannot bear to delay in doing it. It is of these
that the Lord has said: "At the hearing of the ear they have
obeyed me" (Ps 18:44) (RB, 5).

THE FUNDAMENTALS AND GOAL
OF BENEDICTINE OBEDIENCE

Chapter 5 of the Rule opens with the above words. Why? Because: one who speaks of love also speaks of the renunciation of self. The lover could not say to the beloved: "I would like to depend on you" (in order to receive life). Love and the will for independence are not compatible, even on the surface. Obedience makes me renounce myself, and thus favors the union with God. The fundamental idea of obedience—contrary to poverty and chastity—is not found in one of Christ's teachings, but in an attitude he practiced himself, and even more, in what he was.

In John 5:19–20, we find these words: "The Son can do nothing on his own, but only what he sees the Father doing; for whatever the Father does, the Son does likewise. The Father loves the Son and shows him all that he himself is doing...." In essence, the Son, the filial bond par excellence, is then not able to do anything of himself, but all that the Father does.

Benedictine obedience then is not to be sought in group life, in the safety of the common good, in the need for a leader who orders the entire life of the community, but because the follower of Benedict's Rule believes that the abbot represents Christ and because the monk has established a relationship with his superior like that of the Son with regard to his Father. The perfection of love is only to want what the other wants. In the Gospel of John, the Lord tells us: "I will always do everything that pleases him" and "I do as the Father has commanded me" (Jn 14:31).

For the follower of the Rule of Benedict, obedience is addressed only to God because it is a renunciation in order to do his (God's) will, to follow the leanings of his inclinations and desires, to organize his life to agree with God in order to be worthy to perceive and discern the will of God: what he sees as good, acceptable, and perfect (Rom 12:2).

God speaks through his commandments, laws, and his authority. But there are also invitations from brothers, councils of the people of God, small and large events, as well as divine inspirations. It is at the cost of perseverant renunciation to God's will that we discern the second way to speak to God. To obey his commandments should lead us to show ourselves receptive to the wishes and suggestions of superiors, spiritual advisors, daily events, and inspirations of the Holy Spirit. The goal of obedience is this: to become docile to the inspirations of the Holy Spirit through renunciation of our own will.

The true goal of obedience is for God to become, in all truth, the sole Master of our will. "For all who are led by the Spirit of God are children of God" (Rom 8:14). On the condition that there is a concrete transformation (always concrete) of our humility, because this obedience—not military, but through love—is the participation in this filial submission, which is a participation in the spirit of Christ with regard to his Father. It shows our interior suppleness under the hand of God.

By relinquishing my own will to another in order to only

want what God wants, as expressed by the superior—even if he is wrong—I will attain the will of God for me: a participation in the dependence of the Son on the Father, a participation in the bowing-down of the Son before the Father, an imitation of the bowing-down of Phil 2:6, to be moved by the Holy Spirit. God remains the master of our destinies, in spite of the secondary causes which could be defective (the superiors). That is why the order is not necessarily the best, but it becomes the best for those who are interested.

By obeying, we embrace the will of God, but the will of God cannot be separated from God, it is one and the same. Obedience is not an annihilation of the person or of his freedom, but the highest concretization. The monk unites his will to God's will. But obedience could appear to be an obstacle to fulfillment. In reality, it is obedience that provides it, if it is practiced through love (see RB, 68). It gives us a permanent disposition with regards to the divine will, which is the quality of love. Then, the soul that is freed of its own will can allow God to work in it.

QUALITIES OF BENEDICTINE OBEDIENCE

But this obedience will only be acceptable to God, and agreeable to the human person, if the order is executed without trouble, without delay, without resistance, without comment, and without words of resistance. For obedience rendered to superiors is obedience rendered to God, as he said: "He who hears you, hears me," and it is willingly that disciples must obey because God loves those who give joyously.

Saint Benedict comes back in Chapter 68 to the subject of obedience where he foresees the case when a brother is asked to do an impossible task:

If a brother is requested to do something difficult or impossible he should, at first, accept the command meekly and obediently. If he sees that the task is beyond his means, respectfully, calmly, and humbly, he will tell his superior the reason for it. He will not be proud, resistant, or contradictory. If, however, after these representations, the superior insists on his command, let the subject be persuaded that it will be to his benefit, and let him obey out of love, trusting in the help of God.

If the superior keeps to his decision despite the brother's reasons, the brother in charity will do as told, trusting in God's help.

There is then a time for a discussion with authorities; this time is brought to an end by the superior, then in the midst of interior agitation, the disciple should force himself to listen to his heart and obey. Once again, this obedience is suitable for "all who think of Christ above all else." The word "obey" comes from the Latin word "audire," which means to listen. We come back, once again, to listening to God. This time it is to win over our own will, that is, our egoism.

REFLECTION QUESTIONS

Though we are not bound to the discipline of the monastic life, and do not share in its method of molding obedience through an abbot representative of Christ, we are called to obey our Lord just as those monks are called to do. But who can serve as our guide? For the sake of stricter obedience to the will of Christ, can I seek out a spiritual director—a priest from a nearby parish, a nun from a local convent—to assist me on my journey to deeper obedience to the will of God? Can I take the time from my day and pray on what it means to be truly obedient, and what it is Christ is calling me to do?

Saint Benedict mentions humility hand-in-hand with obedience. Do I seek these two twin virtues and then use them to form a solid and unwavering outlook that promotes the love of God? How am I able to promote obedience and humility in the context of my own circumstances? When I ascertain the will of God, do I follow it promptly, or am I a malingerer who puts off my obligation? What ways do I use to avoid following God's expectations for me? What false justifications do I cling to in order not to acknowledge the full reluctance of my obedience?

DAY FIVE

Humility

FOCUS POINT

True humility is the path to true love. Just as Christ humbled himself, taking the form of a slave, living his life in humble obedience to the Father, we are called to place the lives of others and the will of God above our own desire and will. We must inspect our lives in every detail, rooting out those elements that are prideful and afraid, those darker corners, and offer them up to God for purification. We seek to love and not to count the cost. For if it costs us our selfishness, what have we really lost?

Holy Scripture proclaims to us, brothers: "Everyone who exalts himself shall be humbled, and he who humbles himself shall be exalted" (Lk 14:11). In saying this, it teaches us that all exaltation is of the nature of pride, which vice the prophet shows that he took care to avoid, saying: "O Lord, my heart is not proud, nor are my eyes raised too high; I have not occupied myself with things too great and too marvelous for me" (Ps 131:1). And why? "For if I were not humble, but had exalted my soul, as a child that is weaned from its mother, so would my soul likewise be rewarded" (Ps 131:2).

If we wish to reach the highest peak of humility and soon arrive at the heavenly heights, we must, by our good deeds, set up a ladder like Jacob's, upon which he saw angels climbing up and down. Without doubt, we should understand that climbing as showing us that we go up by humbling ourselves and down by praising ourselves. The ladder represents our life in the temporal world; the Lord has erected it for those of us possessing humility. We may think of the sides of the ladder as our body and soul, the rungs as the steps of humility and discipline we must climb in our religious vocation (RB 7).

THE LADDER OF HUMILITY

In the Benedictine Rule, Chapter 7 is the most important. After having seen that it is necessary to return to God, and showing us the instruments of good works in order to truly seek God, Saint Benedict deals with the characteristic that is the key to Benedictine asceticism: humility.

For the monk, the first step of humility consists of developing a very real sense of God in his soul, a feeling of the transcendence and of the "tremendum" and "fascinosum" mystery. Benedict's God is not a companion God. This step is

a placing of oneself into the presence of God. In the language
of the abbot of Monte Cassino, it is the "fear of God." One
does not ignore God. The monk will judge that "God up above
sees him at all times and in all cases looks upon him from the
divinity gained from his actions." We are reminded that
Benedict, in Subiaco, lived "under the scrutiny of the loving
eyes of the eternal Heedful One, the Great Witness," "wanting to only please God." From whence comes this vigilance?

In Chapter 4, Benedict stated: "to monitor one's actions
ceaselessly." To monitor means to pay attention to what one
says and does and to carry the light of conscience in our actions. But how do we give them light?

Saint Benedict answered, "be assured that God sees us everywhere," and also, "beg of Him to finish the good work
begun"(RB, Prologue), that is to say: before doing any good
deed, ask Christ, and do this asking from the most intimate
part of yourself, so that you may accomplish this deed in imitation of his perfection. We can see the practice of this teaching and the Lord's promise in John 14:13: "I will do whatever
you ask in my name, so that the Father may be glorified in the
Son." It is not enough just to want to do the deed, not only to
want it, but to do it. And that action comes from grace, for as
Saint Paul said: "For it is God who is at work in you, enabling
you both to will and to work for his good pleasure" (Phil 2:13).

Saint Benedict also took great care to mention, still in Chapter 4, "to attribute to God the good one sees and oneself; to
recognize that the evil in oneself is attributable only to oneself."

It is therefore necessary to cease being the owners of our
actions in order to attribute and perform them, according to
Saint Paul's formula: "in Christ." In India, a swami would say,
"de-individualize yourself." Thus, everything will be done in

the light of day, that is to say, through faith, in the light of a conscience that is united with that of Christ.

If we remain the owners of our actions, if we believe that we alone accomplish them and not him within us and through us, we are in a state of spiritual sleep. We won't know what evil we could do. Our awakening has not been realized, for Christ said: "...apart from me, you can do nothing" (Jn 15:5).

To this feeling of acute faith, the monk adds the denial of his own will. The second step (of humility) is this:

> [T]hat a man love not his own will nor delight in grati-fying his own desires, but carry out in his deeds that saying of the Lord: "I came not to do my own will but the will of him who sent me" (Jn 6:38). And again Scripture says: "Self-will has punishment but necessity wins a crown."

The follower of the Rule acts in such a way that God's will is substituted for his own, to do not one's own will, but the will of the Father. Submission to the superior through obedi-ence for the love of God in imitation of the Lord is what the apostle referred to when he said: "He humbled himself and became obedient to the point of death" (Phil 2:8). This is the model of the third step of humility. This obedience is imposed on the monk, even in "difficulties and austerities" (RB, 58).

In the midst of adversities, the follower of Benedict's Rule is supported by the hope of divine reward, "for in all these things, we are more than conquerors through him who loved us" (Rom 8:37). That is the nugget of the fourth step of humility:

> The fourth degree of humility is, that if, in this very obedience, hard and contrary things, even injuries, are

done to a person, he should take hold silently on patience, and, bearing up bravely, grow not weary or depart, according to the saying of the Scripture: "But the one who endures to the end will be saved" (Mt 10:22).

The fifth step is the opening of the conscience to the Spiritual Father about which we have already spoken. The sixth step is reached when the monk contentedly accepts all that is crude and harsh and thinks of himself as a poor and worthless worker in his appointed task, saying with the prophet: "I was stupid and ignorant; I was like a brute beast toward you. Nevertheless I am continually with you; you hold my right hand" (Ps 73: 22–23).

The seventh step is arrived at when the monk not only confesses that he is inferior, but also believes it with the inmost feeling of his heart, humbling himself and saying with the prophet: "I am a worm, and not human; scorned by others, and despised by the people" (Ps 22:6).

The eighth step is achieved when a monk only does that which is the common rule of the monastery or what the example of the elders demands. All individuality flees, and the monk becomes detached even from the choice of what means are to be used in the pursuit of perfection. The common custom of the monastery is that it is to be the guide, and conformance to the best elements of the community are to be practiced within its walls. As Chapter 3 of the Rule states:

> Let all, therefore, follow this rule as their guide, and let no one decline from it rashly. Let no one in the monastery follow the promptings of his own heart, neither should anyone presume insolently to contend with his Abbot either within or without the monastery.

The ninth step is the practice of silence. The monk restrains his tongue from speaking and maintains silence, only speaking when he is asked a question. This practice is supported by Scripture, which teaches: "When the words are many, transgression is not lacking, but the prudent are restrained in speech" (Prov 10:19). Indeed, speech should always be used sparingly.

The tenth step is reached when a monk refrains from laughter or frivolity—as silence is the rule of monastic life. This practice follows Scripture which says that it is the fool who lifts up his voice in laughter.

Does the monk speak at all? He must speak gently, seriously, with carefully chosen words, barely above a whisper— that is the eleventh step. The follower of the Rule must speak with humility and reason, using as few words as possible.

Finally, in the twelfth step, Benedict asks that a monk show humility in his appearance and actions: he must think of his sins, head down, eyes to the ground, and imagine that he is on trial before God, ever mindful of the words of Luke: "Lord, I, a sinner, am not worthy to raise my eyes to heaven"(Lk 18:13), and "I am utterly bowed down and prostrate; all day long I go around mourning" (Ps 38:6).

In the next chapter, we will see just to what degree and depth one must interpret—and live—these steps of humility. Here, in this chapter, we are reminded of much that can be accomplished through the help of communal grace. Later, we will provide more mystical reading material, for there is a certain mystery in humility that consists of joining Christ in his humbleness.

The retreat participant will then ask for humility, the foundation of all things spiritual, insofar as humility is an incomparable diagnostic tool for taking stock of what is the state of one's soul, for it is the true self.

To have the experience that one is truly nothing could only be the work of God within us, as we will see in the next chapter. This work of God within us is most often realized by the intermediation of the events that happen to us. We are shattered. The sense of "me" has taken such a "slap in the face," especially in steps 6 and 7 that it no longer is deployed. From then on, the person is hidden (steps 8 through 12), and Benedict uses the example of the tax collector in the gospel.

CHRIST, THE FOUNDATION OF HUMILITY

Humility hasn't really been given any "good reviews." Why do we put it down so that the word "Christian" is equated with an inferiority complex?

An inferiority complex is a cartoon representation of true humility. Basically, it is a subtle disguise for pride. We don't act because we don't want to be deceived. Humility—true humility—is realizing that we can do nothing on our own and that it is Christ who does everything within us. The humble soul does not fear taking action and realizing great things, for it seeks to glorify God. The humble soul knows the parable of the Talents (Mt 25:14–30), and, through experience, it knows just how true the teaching of Christ is: "apart from me, you can do nothing" (Jn 15:5). Humility does not debase human beings for it allows them to unite with God. Also, it is "profitable."

Why is so much humbleness necessary? Why must one descend in order to climb? Because of Christ's kenosis. "Who, though he was in the form of God, did not regard equality with God as something to be exploited, but emptied himself, taking the form of a slave, being born in human likeness. And being found in human form, he humbled himself and became obedient to the point of death—even death on a cross. There-fore God also highly exalted him and gave him the name that is above every name" (Phil 2:6–9). And why is there this move-ment of descent and elevation in Christ himself? Because the basis of humility is love itself. A soul that loves will always be humble before the beloved because it wants to take and re-ceive everything from the beloved. To love is to take a backseat to the other, to want good for them even to the detriment of one's own being.

If God has chosen to descend for us through the humble-ness of the Incarnation, it was done so that we are incited to take the same path in order to elevate ourselves all the way to divinization.

That is the reason why if we want to climb, climb higher and yet even higher, we must descend, and descend again. We must make ourselves as small as God will allow us through all of the events of his doing, through the actions of whatever hands he may use to this end. In this way we will keep our-selves open to God's actions upon us.

Think, then, on these things.

The fruit of humility is charity—one draws the other.

Humility leads to the blossoming of charity.

We must then welcome the divine gift of humility.

This symbol of descent is Jacob's ladder—the figure of a mystical life.

Humility is the participation in Christ's sufferings through patience, a mystical participation in all the meanings of humil-ity and Benedictine obedience, bound together with the mys-teries of incarnation and redemption that the monk is called to live. The different steps of the ladder are Saint Benedict's theology of the cross. We climb (in humility) by descending (through "humiliations"). At each step of purification, there is a corresponding new step of Life. The monk dies to himself, step by step, in order to reach the summit of the ladder, this state of mystical death of the self, for humility kills and empties the self. This emptying of self leads us to think of a similar Zen principle.

REFLECTION QUESTIONS

Do I pray regularly for God's grace of humility in my life? Do I regularly acknowledge that without God's grace, without God's very presence in my life, I would be unable to do a single thing? That I would not even exist? Do I recognize how small I am, my creatureliness? Does this recognition instill within me a greater "fear of God," a deeper sense of awe for God's greatness as Creator and Lord?

DAY SIX

More Humility

FOCUS POINT

To recognize one's nothingness as a creature is to grow in holiness with God. To arrive at the awareness that one cannot take credit for anything without fully crediting God, is to recognize one's true state—a creature dependent on the Creator for every aspect of one's life. This humility is the path to "right living" with God, living in a relationship without illusion, without pride. It is a relationship of faith and trust, awe and love.

The sixth step of humility is reached when a monk contentedly accepts all that is crude and harsh and thinks himself a poor and worthless worker in his appointed tasks. He must say with the prophet, "I have been brought to nothing, and did not know it. I have become like a beast before you, and I am always with you" (Ps 73:22–23).

The seventh step of humility is attained when a man not only confesses that he is an inferior and common wretch but believes it in the depths of his heart. He will humble himself and say, with the prophet, "I am a worm and no man, the reproach of men and the outcast of the people" (Ps 22:6) (RB, 7).

A DEEPER LOOK AT CHAPTER 7

Humanly speaking, how can we reconcile the two extremes of happiness and contentment with abasement? How can we come to an opinion of ourselves in which we judge ourselves as being unworthy and incapable of anything?

Could not such personal devaluations bring psychological conflicts and serious depression to some individuals? If we want to truly "stick" to Saint Benedict's text and its practical meaning, that which presupposes, in most cases, slander, scorn, a campaign of denigration, opposition, and persecution—for there is no humility without humiliations, and no holiness without humility—if we want to keep ourselves from "sweetening" our reference text with pious reflections, we must take our cue from asceticism.

In the sixth and seventh steps, the soul sees itself from God's perspective in order to judge itself, for it is precisely on the path of perpetual communion with God, after having experienced the purifying and illuminating paths. What it sees as great in itself—for not knowing how to recognize God's gifts within it would be false humility (see Saint Thomas' *Summa Theologica* IIa, IIae, 161, art. 3)—evidently appears as a work of God for which it has judged to have attributed very little merit. Just the opposite, all of its worries appear so much its own that, with respect to others, it is confused. It will always choose to go and seek the last row, the last place—why? Because this attitude would be the most adapted to its nothingness. "The one who descends will arise." Then the soul will like to recognize its nothingness because this acknowledged nothingness leaves it completely void and open to God. But such a perception of nothingness is only possible thanks to a very particular influence of God on the soul, which, in mystical language, is called the passive night of the spirit. There, it is no longer the soul that acts in order to put itself in its true place, but it is God himself who shows its nothingness to the soul: "I have been brought to nothing, and did not know it. I have become like a beast before you, and I am always with you" (Ps 73:22–23). In other words, the soul touches on an access to holiness. Therefore, the sixth step is the love of one's nothingness before God. The soul perceives the totality of God and the nothingness of the creature. It acquires a profound sense of God's grandeur and his transcendence.

No one could know the immensity of God's sacrifice when he incarnated himself in his Christ, but in its own manner the soul would like to continue his kenosis. There is a propensity in it to let something of this supreme abasement come alive again, according to its own modality. Then everything is in place in order to be reduced to nothing.

HOLINESS

But this isn't all of it. The seventh step changes the person to
the suffering servant in Isaiah (53:3, 10, 11): "He was despised
and rejected by others...a man of suffering and acquainted
with infirmity...he was despised and we held him of no account.... Yet it was the will of the Lord to crush him with
pain.... Out of his anguish he shall see the light and he shall
find satisfaction through his knowledge." By citing, "But I am
a worm and not human; scorned by others and despised by the
people" (Ps 22:6), Saint Benedict meant that the monk was
rejected by human beings and by the most vile of creatures. He
wanted to show that he had become abject, an object of scorn.
In effect, the person saw himself as nothing to the point that
he was nothing in the eyes of God. He allowed the purifying
hand do its work in him. He believed himself capable of all
possible declines from grace and he was. He gave himself the
conviction, the intimate persuasion that he was the most
scorned of all men. The divine light enlightens and "he believed in that from the bottom of his heart." Without the loving
recognition of his nothingness, humility would not be complete. To recognize one's nothingness without wanting to show
it is not the humility of heart that our Lord recommended.
The seventh step is therefore the love of our nothingness before humankind. The monk must love to recognize what he is,
because recognized nothingness leaves a void in him so that
God may completely full him up. He sees—this is what makes
him happy—that everything that is good in him comes from
God, that it is God who did it in him and through him. God
has truly become everything.

Humility makes a void in the soul, but charity fills it in.
"When a monk has climbed all twelve steps, he will find that
perfect love of God which casts out fear, by means of which

everything he had observed anxiously before will now appear simple and natural. He will no longer act out of the fear of hell, but for the love of Christ, out of good habits and with a pleasure derived of virtue. The Lord, through the Holy Spirit, will show this to His servant, cleansed of sin and vice" (RB, 7).

Then the soul loves God for himself. Now, the search for his own interests become the interests of God. The effort spent to acquire virtue, his perception of his own progress, his merits and the rewards he expects—all of that is finished. The person acts through the love of Christ. Here, he acts through a passive love that is very pure and perfect. Humility has lead to perfect charity.

"The Lord, through the Holy Spirit, will show this to His servant, cleansed of sin and vice" (RB, 7). The twelve steps of humility are twelve steps of love. "It is good for me that you have humbled me, so that I may learn your statutes" (Ps 119:71). Through this, he perceives a greater love that purifies daily.

In the twelfth step, the monk must, at all times, "think of his sins, head down, eyes on the ground" (RB, 7). His model is the tax collector in the gospel. Why him? It is because Saint Benedict had arrived at this highest step of humility—the highest summit of holiness—and he spoke of "his little rule, written for beginners." In fact, this passage from Chapter 73, "you will come to the heights of doctrine and virtue under God's guidance," does not only aim at the teachings of the Holy Fathers, whether it is Basil or those in the desert, but Benedict aims his Chapter 7 here, especially steps 6, 7, and 12, in fact, to the highest holiness. At the top of the ladder, the soul voided of itself is invaded by the Holy Spirit. That is verified in our last chapter.

REFLECTION QUESTIONS

To arrive at humility is to live in reality. Do I recognize my nothingness as a creature? Do I realize that every facet of my existence depends upon God? Am I comfortable giving everything in my life over to God? Am I aware of the void that humility leaves in my soul? The absence of pride, the absence of fear. Do I seek to fill that void with charity? Do I pray to God for this charity to fill my life?

DAY SEVEN

Renunciation

FOCUS POINT

When a sculptor shapes his sculpture, he does so by removing superfluous parts of clay from a previously amorphous lump. The true beauty of the piece is revealed by taking away those areas that hide what is meant to be. In much the same manner, in our spiritual life, we attempt to remove those parts of our person that prevent a full relationship of love with God. We try to strip away the selfishness and the fear that hinder our ability to live and love as God wills. These hindrances can be overcome by God's grace.

Let no one presume to give or to receive anything without leave of the Abbot, or to keep anything as his own, absolutely anything at all: either a book or a writing tablet or a pen or

anything whatsoever; since they are to have not even their
bodies or their wills in their own keeping.

They may, however, expect to receive from the Father of
the monastery all that is necessary; but they may not keep what
the Abbot has not given or permitted. Let all things be com-
mon to all, as it is written, but let no one call anything his own
or claim it as such (RB, 33).

WHY RENOUNCE?

The doctrinal foundation of poverty is Christ's call: "If you
wish to be perfect, go, sell all your possessions, and give the
money to the poor...then come, follow me" (Mt 19:21).

But renunciation was not espoused to identify a monk with
an impoverished milieu to better proclaim the Good News,
nor for economic or community reasons; it was because Christ
himself was poor—that Christ received his entire being, everything he had, from the Other, that he wanted to have received
everything from the Father. Therefore, renunciation is required.

Benedictine poverty is a poverty of dependence, a dependence upon the Father of the monastery. The disciple would
therefore be in the same relationship as Christ had with respect to his Father. Someone who lives in the spirit of poverty
has his trust in God. Nothing prevents him from giving of himself totally to the actions of the One who comes to him. No
temptation of self-sufficiency—pride—is to be feared since he
possesses nothing on which to establish the least sufficiency.
He could only depend upon God for everything. The soul is
always marveled by the way God treats it. It lives the Word of

God: "Do not worry about your life, what you will eat, or about your body, what you will wear" (Lk 12:22). And if, at times, God leaves us with a degree of uncertainty about tomorrow, we remember that it is our way of communing with the world's problems and espousing what two-thirds of humanity is forced to live with—want.

Even though renunciation is a characteristic of Benedictine spirituality, Chapter 31 of the Rule dealing with the duties of the cellarer makes the effort to describe that no one should be troubled or saddened in the house of the Lord and it underlines that one must look upon all of the goods that belong to the monastery as if they are the sacred vessels of the altar.

Monks must hope and expect to receive what is necessary from the Father of the monastery, for Chapter 34 of Benedict's Rule directs that distribution is to be made to each one according to his need. Accordingly, when someone requires less, let him give thanks to God and not be distressed; when, however, a person requires more, let him be humble in the face of his need and not become arrogant because of the charity given to him. But whatever is in surplus is to be taken away (see RB, 55).

MATERIAL AND SPIRITUAL POVERTY

We have always made a distinction between the two types of poverty, spiritual and material. Yet the material type is a function of the spiritual. It is impossible to be detached from earthly goods unless we are detached from ourselves. Our love for our neighbor is an indication of our love for God, a little like our humility before others is an indication of our humility before God.

Within ourselves, poverty has no value. That which spiritualizes a person is the poverty that is accepted, sought after and desired through love for Jesus. It is the desire to imitate Jesus as much as possible, in order to better belong to him. It is not subjected poverty, but a real and loved poverty. Pascal said it all in a famous phrase: "I love poverty because Jesus loved it."

What does it mean to really live in poverty? Poverty is a simplification of life. It is a reduction of one's needs and an exclusion of what is superfluous. The poverty that was preached by Jesus had a certain indifference to material goods; it is the Paulist who says: "...those who buy as though they had no possessions, and those who deal with the world as though they had no dealings with it. For the present form of the world is passing away" (1 Cor 7:30–31). In India, we say that this affection for possessions is "maya," an illusionary fascination.

We are content with what is necessary and in order to obtain it, we rely upon the heavenly Father, who gives us our work. The heart is elsewhere, rather than hooked on the goods of this life, because our treasure is in heaven. In brief, it is to be content with a little, just with what is necessary. Then God will become the only treasure of the soul. Poverty presupposes that all personal property would be decided upon and dependent on another. It is connected to obedience and humility.

Is it necessary to go all the way to destitution? No. The best form of religious poverty for the Benedictine tradition is not one that implies the greatest destitution, but one which best separates all concern with regard to earthly goods from the one most apt to nourish the virtue of hope and render one rich with God. To sum it up, a reminder of Saint Paul's words: "Piety is happy with that which is necessary" (see 1 Tim 6:6). However, we must note that what is necessary varies for each person and with the degree of their union with God. If we need more, we humble ourselves. If we need less, we do not rouse indignation in those who have more, but we will be cognizant of the Lord and be satisfied with less.

Material poverty aims at our property, but there is also spiritual poverty which not only consists in the detachment from the things of this world, but also in the deprivation of one's self in order to allow God to fill the place that was occupied by our "me." It aims at not preferring or attaching oneself to temporal goods: rank, pride, duties; or natural goods: health, intelligence, talents, judgment; or sensory goods: satisfaction, reputation, relationships, desires for certain functions; or moral goods: virtues, merits; or supernatural goods: consolations, distinctive graces, places of prayer. "Having nothing yet possessing everything" (2 Cor 6:10).

Therefore we will have to examine ourselves with respect to all that is superfluous which may be in our lives. All that we will find to be more than necessary must be removed. The theme of Saint Benedict's Chapter 55 is really summed up in "that is enough."

REFLECTION QUESTIONS

What are those parts of me that I seek to shed that keep me from loving God as I would like? How can they be removed? What efforts can I make—with the grace of God—to focus more directly on a life lived for God, rather than a life lived for me? How can humility serve to clean out this selfish space and fill it with charity? Do I recognize the deep desire in myself to rest in the trust of God rather than exhaust myself in the illusion of self-sufficiency?

DAY EIGHT

Other People

FOCUS POINT

The presence of Christ is present in all those people we encounter in our lives. We, the Church, are the Body of Christ on earth. We love our brothers and sisters because we see God in each one of them, and because each one of them is called to love God. In many ways we are able to show our love for God by serving his creatures in humility and love, just as he taught us when he walked the earth as a humble servant.

Just as there is an evil zeal of bitterness that separates us from God and leads to hell, so there is a good spirit of zealousness which keeps one from vice and leads to God and eternal life. Monks should practice this zeal with ardent love. Let them, "in honor anticipate one another" (Rom 12:10). Let them accept each other's frailties (of body or soul). Let them try to outdo each other in obedience. Let no one do what is best for himself, but rather what is best for another. Let them expend the charity of brotherhood in chaste love. Let them love their abbot with sincerity and humility. Let them fear God and think of nothing before Christ, who can lead us to eternal life (RB, 72).

Fraternal charity is difficult, very difficult. Saint Benedict did not give a ladder for fraternal charity as he did for humility because, for him, humility is connected with charity. Here, though, is a suggested twelve steps of charity to study in conjunction with the twelve steps of humility.

A HOLY LADDER

The first step of charity is to accept that my brother, sister, or spouse has at least one fault.

The second step is to admit that my brother, sister, or spouse has at least two faults.

The third step is to accept that, in the light of human weakness, we have at least one fault ourselves.

The fourth step is to bear the criticisms of our friends and, in spite of exaggerations, to profit from them. In order to do that, one must calm one's imagination, slow down one's heartbeats, and keep quiet.

The fifth step is to recognize that our brother has at least one quality.

The sixth step is to recognize that our brother has at least two qualities.

The seventh step consists of trying to acquire the qualities we see in others.

The eighth step is to try to discover Christ in the qualities of our brothers.

The ninth step is to discover Christ behind the faults and sins of our brothers.

The tenth step is to not judge our brothers and thus not to demolish them.

The eleventh step is not only to not make yourself a nuisance to them, but to seek their well-being.

The twelfth step is to forgive others, those who have made us suffer. We must go to that extent, for the Lord said: "Be perfect, therefore, as your heavenly Father is perfect" (Mt 5:48).

But it is clear that forgiveness is in the will, not in the mind, nor in the senses.

We must accept that our brothers will be something other than figments of our imagination. I must also be something other than I imagine myself to be. We want others to be like what we would like them to be. They are not like that, that is a deception. But to understand is to forgive.

"JUST AS I HAVE LOVED YOU" (JN 13:34).

Jesus loves us in spite of our faults. It is not necessary to be complacent about the existence of sin in the world, about the darkness which is found in beings. But it is necessary to, once and for all, let this capital truth of the gospel enter into our spirit and heart: our misery does not stop God from loving us infinitely; similarly, others' miseries should not stop us from loving them as God loves them. "Just as you did it to one of the least of these who are members of my family, you did it to me" (Mt 25:40). This is a phrase that we must always remember and meditate on. It is not to only withstand the faults of others, to not be surprised at their weaknesses, to edify the acts of virtue we see them do, but to want good for them, to promote their ascension, to make them happy in the little things like in greater ones.

By loving God in our neighbor, by loving him for God, we love him for himself in that most personal of areas: his fundamental relationship with God, his aspirations towards God which identifies him with his own vocation, and those that appear to me to be far removed are potentially the members of the Body of Christ. Also, our vision of our neighbor must be without illusion and full of love.

This is what is the result of a life that is led in communion as Saint Benedict wanted. A community is founded on mutual forgiveness. The patriarch of the monks in his brevity did not say all of that, but, "If we love one another, God lives in us, and his love is perfected in us" (1 Jn 4:12).

REFLECTION QUESTIONS

Am I able to see beyond the faults of my brothers and sisters, and love them for who they are, children of God? Am I able to identify qualities in my brothers and sisters that might benefit my relationship with God, and pray that God might strengthen these qualities in me for the sake of my spiritual life? Do I make an effort to live in communion with God while I live in community with other people? Do I see the parallels between those two relationships?

DAY NINE

Welcome

FOCUS POINT

Monasteries are centers of prayer, and monks are seekers of God. It can be a transforming experience for a layperson to visit a monastery and see seekers of God living according to a rule of life. Similarly, we can provide an excellent example to those around us, as we live our lives as seekers of God. We may not live according to a rule or vow obedience to an abbot, but we can live lives in which God is our center. And we can welcome all those who we encounter to share in our love for God.

Let all guests arriving at the monastery be welcomed as Christ himself, because He said, "I was a stranger, and you took me in" (Mt 25:35). Let due honor and special care be paid to all, especially to those who are of the household of the faith and to strangers.

When, therefore, a guest is announced, let him be met by the superior or by the brothers with all marks of charity. Let them first pray together and then give the kiss of peace; but this kiss of peace must not be given without prayer having first been said, because of the delusions of the devil.

In the salutation itself let all humility be shown. Both on their arrival and on their departure, Christ, who is indeed received, shall be worshiped in all the guests by an inclination of the head or a full prostration of the body. After the guests have been received, let them be led to prayer, and then let the superior, or one authorized by him, sit with them; let the Divine Law be read before the guest that he may be edified; and then let all kindness be shown to him.... Let the Abbot pour water on the hands of the guest; and both he and he whole community shall wash the feet of all the guests. After this washing, let them say: "We have received your mercy, O God, in the midst of your Temple" (Ps 47:9). Let great care and solicitude be shown particularly in the reception of the poor and of travelers, because it is in them that Christ is more especially received. (RB, 53).

THE TRUE MEANING
OF BENEDICTINE HOSPITALITY

Tradition has always unanimously presented monasticism in the light of what we now call a vertical dimension of Christianity; or as being the purest expression of a movement of transcendence. That is what the first monks sought by leaving the Christian communities for the desert: the confession of divine transcendence, the absolute for the absolute, not the absolute for man, to live for God alone. In the time that followed the era of persecution, the desert was the ultimate consequence for the requirements of Christian asceticism, with the goal of better confessing the transcendence of God. But nothing is said that today, given the flux of the world which has different structures from those of yesteryear, but which also remains and is even perhaps more removed from God, doesn't lead us to another ultimate consequence: to show the transcendent God through the witness of our life, to be the revealers of God's love, of the meaning of life and creation. The horizontal relationship of the monastic vocation, the relationship with the mystical body must be stressed more than ever before. Elsewhere, at the time of discoveries and voyages, the desert could only be a relative term. Where can we find such a place today, one that is difficult to reach by automobile? And today, demons live everywhere, not only in the desert, but in the midst of the people who live without hope and without God. Without taking anything away from that which constitutes monasticism, having seen the conjuncture of the present and the future, the monks must be witnesses of divine transcendence, through a detachment from created things and from their values, even if they are good, out of love for God, in order to reach the zone of their most profound being, that which is in God.

Modern atheism is very prevalent because man has become too great and also because man now has a vivid awareness of what he is. God also appears impossible and alienating. The monk shows that man without God is cut off, that God completes man. In order to make man grow, it is not necessary—

just the opposite is true—to reject God. Therefore, the monk is the person, who, faced with generalized indifference, shows God and the grandeur of man to our civilization of tomorrow.

In order to give a true meaning to this world that is being born, to lead it towards that which is its final destiny, to show that the most impressive technique only touches the surface and not its profound being, we must reveal the dimension of depth to man, make him discover the interior experience. In order for this to occur, certain persons must live one-to-one in plenitude. Certain persons must concentrate on adoration. Monasteries are just as essential as factories.

The monks who want to be men of God above all must show themselves to humanity as being on the path towards the end days, towards which humankind is going. It is therefore desirable that the monastic experience be close at hand. In order for this to happen, it must open itself to the real needs of the civilization to come.

THE APOSTOLATE OF THE MONASTERIES

It is normal for us to want to visit a center that seeks God. That is what a monastery is, nothing more: a center to seek God. A monk is nothing other that a seeker of God. As the one who is specialized in the monastic search for God ploughs the field which is written about in the gospel—that field that he purchased in exchange for all the goods of this world—he discovers, little by little, always more and in a better way, the treasure that is hidden there.

Monks should want to give this pearl that Jesus also spoke about to their brothers, to those who want to come to them, to those who want to share their life of prayer for a few hours or days. All those who want to learn to pray are welcome. The monks have riches for all miseries, remedies for all ills.

Today, a truth is not accepted until it is verified by experience. That is why all experiences belong to the entire world; the experience of a milieu of spiritual life must be accessible. And one of the grandeurs of today's world is that it does come to find out about this monastic life experience, right where it is lived.

Monasteries must play a pivotal role in the construction of the Christian people. Not only just short visits, but individual and group retreats are now organized in monasteries and retreat centers. We must reflect and ask ourselves if it wouldn't be beneficial for us to stop and spend some time in one of these centers that seek God, to help feed ourselves from the life-giving source, or even go there through simple curiosity. More and more, the monastic life proposes interesting experiences in collaboration or association with lay people, all the way to a certain integration into the monastery: the oblates. This is the result of a long history that finds its roots in Chapter 59 of the Rule. Saint Benedict's proposal of "think of nothing before Christ who can lead us into eternal life," of Chapter 72, takes on a fuller meaning in our current times. Does not our welcome to our brother and sister provide proof of the opening of our heart to God? And didn't Saint Benedict tell us that when we play the host in this way, we are welcoming Christ himself? That is why those who like to pray with Benedict will voluntarily receive their friends, work associates, neighbors, and the poor. As always, it is necessary to listen to what the Lord wants to tell us through them.

REFLECTION QUESTIONS

Do I have time in my schedule to visit a monastery for a weekend retreat? How might such a retreat benefit my spiritual life? If I do not have time for this, how might *I* serve as a place of welcome, as a center for seeking, to whose who enter my life? Do I make strangers feel welcome? Do I attempt to break down the walls that divide me from others? So I see Christ in all who cross my path?

DAY TEN

Peace

─────────

FOCUS POINT

According to Benedict, peace is very much in line with the virtue of temperance. There is a balance that must be maintained if a person is to experience peace. Never too much of one thing; that can upset the balance. True peace has at its heart harmony—each mood and desire occurring at its appropriate time and in its appropriate measure. There are suitable elements of solitude, self-control, modesty, simplicity, gentleness, wisdom, and moderation.

─────────

Seek peace and pursue it (RB, Prologue).

─────────

A CONQUEST, A GIFT

Peace is the sign of Messianic goods in the Old Testament, the fruit of the Holy Spirit according to Saint Paul, the anticipated possession of the kingdom according to the gospel!

How can we have this promised interior peace? How do we partake of this interior equilibrium? What is peace? The tranquility of the order is the result of peace, but peace itself is more than an equilibrium of the forces that are within us, an equilibrium that is always precarious, but which places each and every thing in its proper place. It is a unification of all beings under the auspices of Jesus, "for he is our peace" (Eph 2:14), not only because he has reconciled us with God, man, and ourselves, but because he brings to us the great principle that unifies our life: the circumstances of our childhood, adolescence, and the walk through the shadows of our sometimes chaotic lives, thanks to "the deifying light" of faith.

How do we partake of this unification, not only of our life, but of the zones of our being that are in conflict within ourselves? And so, we must heal the wounds of the soul. In order to come back to ourself, we must accept ourselves with our limitations and accept others. Accept ourselves for what we are. The entire Rule, that is to say the whole body of reflections to lead our life according to Saint Benedict, is ordered on this conquest or on the reception of this gift of interior peace.

We must aim for this at all times, in all places, for righteous thought and action, that is to say that which is appropriate in each circumstance, keeping our temperament in mind. We must know how to discern what leads to God.

To discover what leads to God, in a given circumstance, for a certain determined subject, for a particular speaker, is the fruit of the "discretio," that is to say of a discernment under

God's gaze. It is the righteous choice, it is often the righteous middle ground...which is a summit.

ATTITUDE OF THE SOUL

The proper attitude of soul brings with it a particular bearing.

The monk is serious, even grave, the sign by which we recognize in the heart of a soul the triumph of its unity, the intimate possession of self, the imperturbable freedom. He has peace, the sign that he has found God, the sign that everything is in order within him and in his life, the sign of the feeling of unity. He is stable, he has a sense of the possible. He feels that only a thin roof separates him from the great Meeting. That is why he must "see death before him daily" (RB, 4).

Saint Benedict is concerned about the important factors of harmony in the human body: nourishment (RB, 39), sleep in sufficient quantities (RB, 22), and a regular schedule for meals (RB, 41). He wanted the abbot to be a reflection of the goodness of the heavenly Father for his children. Nervousness, mood changes, and impulsiveness are banned from his make-up.

The contingent must play a role, its true role, not absolute but relative, the principle being the present moment and its correspondence to the goal already possessed in the obscure. The richness of the moment which contains God! True peace is given through a penetration into the beyond of ourselves in order to be absorbed there by the light which radiates from the Firstborn. It is the fruit of interior solitude, self-control, the refusal of all agitation, of each thing in its own time. It is the atmosphere which must reign in the training center for service to the Lord.

Order and organization give peace—that is why Saint Benedict loved them so much. It is the intimate feeling that we live with God's will. It is the repose of the soul in unity. Peace means simplicity, modesty, moderation, wisdom, gentleness, and lovability. It is the sign of God's bounty in the soul. It is the serenity of the spirit. Peace at this level is so rare, but it is fitting that the word *peace* is often sighted as the Benedictine motto.

REFLECTION QUESTIONS

There is a peace that comes with discipline. How am I at checking the balance of temperance in my life? Does prayer benefit me in gauging my level of agitation and how to best control it? Do I seek peace? Do I hand over the anxieties, those things I cannot control, to God and allow him to take control? Do I practice centering prayer? Do I pray the "serenity prayer"?

DAY ELEVEN

Liturgy

FOCUS POINT

The center of a monk's life is liturgy; his daily life revolves around liturgy. The liturgy is interiorized by the monk and that liturgy seeks expression. In the same manner, when we leave Mass on Sunday, we are seeking to express the liturgy we have just interiorized. Our forms of expression are myriad, and we begin this expression the moment the priest tells us, "The Mass is ended. Let us go in peace to love and serve the Lord."

We believe that the divine presence is everywhere, and that the eyes of the Lord behold the good and the evil in every place. Especially do we believe this without any doubt when we are assisting at the work of God.

Let us ever remember what the prophet says: "Serve the Lord with fear" (Ps 2:11), and again, "Sing praises to God" (Ps 47:6), and "I give you thanks, O Lord, with my whole heart; before the gods I sing your praise" (Ps 138:1). Therefore let us consider how we ought to conduct ourselves in the presence of God and his angels, and so assist at the Divine Office that our mind may be in harmony with our voice. (RB, 19).

Chapters 8 to 19 of Benedict's Rule are dedicated to the Divine Office, "the work of God," to which nothing must be preferred. The expression "Divine Office" refers to liturgical prayers spread throughout the day in vigils: lauds (morning prayers), prime, tierce (around 10:00 A.M.), sext (noon), none (beginning of the afternoon), vespers (end of the afternoon), and compline (before bed). The Divine Office is made up of a compilation of hymns, psalms, readings, responses, the Our Father, all ending with a prayer and a benediction.

WHAT DOES A MONK DO IN A CHOIR?

When a person sings or recites the Divine Office—there is actually a varied choice of schemas for prayer in the Church—not only must he understand the psalms, but he must also fulfill them. It is Christ who is speaking, singing, suffering, and triumphing in the psalm. However, the Word of God is God himself in the act by which he reveals and communicates himself to us. Through the diversity of all times, a single man, head and body, is built: Christ. The recitation of the Office also teaches the orator to recall the words of Saint Augustine, that "we are Christ in this world," that he lives in Christians and that what has been said of him has been fulfilled and is still being fulfilled in us. That is why, while giving the required attention to the words and gestures in order to humanly express them, the soul can withdraw itself from the multitude of thoughts and feelings that are being expressed in order to unite itself with the presence of God. Quite often, the monk adopts this behavior. "God is everywhere…without a doubt, we believe this is so, especially when assisting in the Divine Office" (RB, 19). Therefore, the first way to celebrate the Divine Office is to pay attention to the divine presence, but let us intone it in such a way that our hearts and voices are in harmony. What was important to Saint Benedict was not so much the psychological attention or critical intelligence given to the sacred text, but that the interior person be united with the divine Word, becoming a single heart with him. Then the profound meaning of this famous phrase in the Benedictine world, cited at the beginning of this chapter, is not found in a certain harmonious vocal interpretation, nor even in an attentive and intelligent intonation, given that this would be included without a doubt as a necessary condition, but is in the living union of our interior being with the Logos that appears in the sacred text. His injured inner self is crucified by this very same teaching which inspires his words; the speaker or singer becomes what he says.

Also, the Divine Office is not like a department in the life of a Benedictine monk; it is literally his life. He is nourished by the liturgy; he blossoms in it because contemplation is the fulfillment of the liturgical act. Prayer interiorizes the mystery and by interiorizing it, it gives it life, but it needs to be projected into the sensory world in order to be interiorized and given life, for that is where liturgy comes from. The projection into the sensory world aims at its interiorization. In order to intensify itself even more and to develop further, interiorizations need to be projected, especially given man's sensual condition. He needs words, signs, and symbols.

CHRIST'S PRAYER TO HIS FATHER

But there is a third way to focus the singing of the psalms. They could be addressed to Christ, as they had, without a doubt, been addressed in this way at the origins of monasticism. They could also be addressed to God. The psalms are addressed through Christ to the Father in a union with all of humankind. In the psalms, we must not listen to the voice of one person in prayer, but to the voice of all of those who are in Christ.

Supported by Saint Paul, Saint Augustine often described Christ and the Church as having a single voice, for it is Christ who prays in us: "He prays for us as our priest, he prays in us as our head, he is prayed to through us as our God. Let us recognize then our words in him and his words in us." Also, said Saint Augustine, "We pray to him when he is in the form of God. He prays in the form of a slave. We speak the prayer of the psalm in him and he speaks in us." Yes, Christ prays in us.

Christ and the Church, the head and the body, that is the mystery of the Scriptures. One head—Christ—who seeks a body—humanity, and one body—humanity—who seeks a head—Christ; this is the complete meaning of the psalms. Also, the doctrine that explains the union between Christ and the Church—thus of each soul—is the great principle for the recitation of the psalms.

Saint Augustine continues: "It is an absolute necessity to think of the totality of Christ (the head and the members) in order to understand the Bible. When Christ speaks, it is at times just the head alone...at times, it is in the name of his Body which is the Church spread across the earth. We are its members. But if one member suffers, all of the members suffer with him. Christ said, today, you are in a state of tribulation, and I am there in tribulation. Tomorrow, another will be in tribulation and I will also be there. Until the end of time, when some member of my body will be in tribulation, I will be there." And, Christ in us battles against "the enemies" of the Psalmist, the forces of evil that are at work in the world.

Let us again cite Saint Augustine: "You rejoice in him since he lives his sadness within you, his suffering within you, his hunger, his thirst within you, his trials within you, he continues to die within you and you within him and you have already been resurrected" (see Ps 103 and PL 37, col. 1284–1285).

Forming only one Body, there is but one Christ to ascend to heaven, but as the head and members. Saint Augustine comments on Christ's words: "I sanctify myself, so that they also may be sanctified in Truth." "It is, he says, so that they may profit from it, since they are also me. And for them, thus, for me, I sanctify myself, that is to say, I sanctify them in myself, like myself, since in me, they also are me." Christians are sanctified in him because he is sanctified by God and they are him.

The person praying the psalms sees, in the recitation of the psalms, all of the trials and all of the joys of humanity. If we have given so much importance to Saint Augustine, it is to show that many riches can come from the Divine Office. Further, we will always have something to gain by reading the Bishop of Hippo's speeches and comments about the psalms, a fountain for better knowledge and greater love for the "work of God."

There is nothing less self-centered than the intoned psalm, since it is the Church's prayer, in which we make all of the requests of the world our own and we praise the Lord for his wonders. We go to God with the words he has inspired. By them, God has praised himself.

Saint Augustine borrows the Lord's words: "When one of my members prays, it is I who is praying"; therefore by praying, one enters, little by little, into Christ's relationship with his Father. The Divine Office is truly the work of God in us; thus any lack of or lapse in this great communal prayer or any delay is difficult to accept.

Liturgy is crowned with the observance of the Eucharist—of which Saint Benedict does not speak, per se—which has taken on an important place in the Benedictine tradition. Therefore, we must make an effort to live by the liturgical calendar of the Church. At the school of Saint Benedict, we become a liturgist. It is through and by the liturgy that the Benedictine monk gets truly in touch with his vocation, because it is in this milieu that he will attain a union with Christ.

The work of praise is so exalted—let us recall that it is the work of God in us, it is God praising himself by the ministry of his incarnate Word and the Church—that it presupposes a moral and ascetic life, that is to say, in Benedictine terms: life conversion (=to live the monastic life as well as possible) and stability (=commitment to the same monastic milieu until death), but all of this program is lived with a spirit of "discretio" (=discernment of what is right for me), "in moderation, though, for the sake of the timorous" (RB, 48), and "never despairing of God's mercy" (RB, 4).

REFLECTION QUESTIONS

Is liturgy a "centering point" in my life? Do I interiorize the liturgy and express that interiorization later on? How do I express it? Through church groups and activities? Through anonymous giving? Through random acts of kindness? When I pray do I feel like I am a part of the larger Mystical Body of Christ that is the Church? Do I see how my prayer—which may seem individually based—is a prayer on behalf of the entire Church?

DAY TWELVE

Reading

FOCUS POINT

There is a dialogue that occurs when one reads the Bible. All spiritual reading should lead to contemplation, to a deeper relationship with our Lord. God speaks to us when we read the Bible, revealing to us the Way, the Truth, and the Life— Jesus Christ. The Bible brings us closer to God, helps us to rely more on him, by making us realize how far from God we really are. We are humbled by its words.

The brothers should be occupied according to schedule in either manual labor or holy reading. We think, therefore, that the times for each may be disposed as follows: from Easter to the fourteenth of September, going forth in the morning, they are to labor at whatever is necessary from the first to about

*the fourth hour. From the fourth until about the sixth hour let
them apply themselves to reading. After the sixth hour, on ris-
ing from table, let them rest on their beds in all silence; or if
perhaps one should wish to read alone, let him so read as not
to disturb anyone else. Let None be said somewhat earlier—at
the middle of the eighth hour; then let them again work at
whatever needs to be done until Vespers (RB, 48).*

Lectio divina, or holy reading, was very important to Saint
Benedict. What does he mean by that?

Lectio divina is a slow and savory period of reading, as if
God was speaking to me himself through the text I am reading. *Lectio divina* was most often done in a loud voice. It is
therefore opposite to our actual way of reading, which quite
often consists of skimming over the text.

THE BIBLE

What did one read? Almost exclusively one read the Bible. But
as time went on, *lectio divina* was extended to include certain
commentaries that have been written by the Fathers of the
Church (RB, 73), and from that extension to include all religious and spiritual books. In the meantime, we are to avoid
books that are too scientific, too scholarly, or exegesis which
does not truly nourish the soul.

The Bible! That is to say, to study the Bible. "It is an inex-
haustible book, it is God's book. We must live in it, get at-
tached to it, and how can we not since it makes the ear of our
heart hear." As Paul Claudel says, the Bible is "the compelling
call of the homeland, of the One who has discovered our deep-

est soul, this forgotten sister." It speaks—as much in the Old as in the New Testament—of only one person, Jesus Christ. It reveals him to us as God's truth, man's truth, and life's truth. It is not a book that is just consulted. It's an adventure in which we follow Jesus.

The Bible makes us hear a call, the call of a God of life. Isn't living a matter of existing while perfecting our being? But by revealing Christ, the Bible reveals myself to me. "I need it to be myself." It will make me realize that I am far from God. It will create a desire within me for the sun, an insatiable desire, and this desire is not only brought on by reading, but it makes it grow, so as to be able to fulfill it one day.

AN OVERTURE TO PRAYER

Scripture is what brings me back to life and unifies me. Through it, I discover my Savior, the one who has the power to grant our most essential desires. It gives access to the bounty of life, the bounty of man is made possible through divinization. The river of the Bible flows through our lives like a constructive force, passing through the destiny of all human beings. It is a story, but it makes each one of us understand our own story, the one written in our soul, so it lets us get in touch with our deepest selves, and to reject and abandon our superficial selves. Each person reads the Bible differently, favoring certain texts, putting others aside. No one reads without interpreting it. It is not a question of gaining knowledge, of deepening our faith, but of allowing God to speak to our hearts.

The Bible is the story of my soul. The Bible is a school of conversion, a school of growth for knowledge of God. "More than that, I regard everything as loss because of the surpassing value of knowing Christ Jesus my Lord" (Phil 3:8). It is existential knowledge which is active since it aims "to know Christ and the power of his resurrection and the sharing of his sufferings" (Phil 3:10).

The Bible is a school of contemplation, a loving and prolonged look at faith: "...you believe in him and rejoice with an indescribable and glorious joy" (1 Pet 1:8). The Bible makes us discover the meaning of the events that have shaped us, and helps us see what we are called to live. Each time we approach it, it becomes an attempt to reread the "proclamation of Jesus Christ, according to the revelation of the mystery that was kept secret for long ages" (Rom 16:25), the knowledge of which each person must discover.

The events of our interior life are then the words of God in the present. A secret dialogue is established between these words and ourselves which the Holy Spirit instigates and which makes an overture to prayer.

REFLECTION QUESTIONS

Do I practice regular spiritual reading? Do I explore different parts of the Bible from time to time in an effort to challenge myself? Do I practice *lectio divina*? How do I view the Bible? As a guide to better living? As a continuing dialogue between myself and God? As a self-revealing text that shows me Christ's presence in the human person?

DAY THIRTEEN

Prayer

FOCUS POINT

When we pray we put ourselves in the presence of God. We meditate on ideas, mysteries, or biblical texts. We realize our love for God in prayer, and God's great love for us, his creation. Prayer is a discipline we must nourish and nurture, especially during periods of dryness in our prayer life. God always calls us to pray.

If one wishes to pray alone at some other time, he will simply go to the oratory and do so silently, with tears and heartfelt fervor (RB, 52).

If, when we wish to bring anything to the notice of a person of high station, we do so with humility and reverence, how much more ought we to offer our supplication to the Lord

God in all humility and purity of devotion. Let us remember that we shall be heard not because of much speaking, but for our purity of heart and tears of compunction. Therefore, prayer ought to be short and pure, unless by chance it is prolonged by the inspiration of Divine Grace. In community, however, let prayer always be short (RB, 20).

WHAT IS PRAYER?

Prayer is breathing, nourishment, thirst, conversation, a glance, a desert, a wall, a never-ending plane, a joy which is not of this world.

It is the burning bush, a sunbath.

It is a gift, a gift for which we often pay dearly. Also, we must ask to receive this gift. The gospel says, "For everyone who asks receives, and everyone who searches finds, and for everyone who knocks, the door will be opened" (Mt 7:8). We must have the conviction that it is necessary and that it is fruitful.

Prayer is thinking about someone we love. For Benedict, it was putting himself in the presence of God. "He hears everything we say to him, and also sees what we think" (see RB, 7). It is useless to use a great many words. Quite often, it brings with it a taste for "coming back for a visit" after times when we are distracted, feeling empty, or of having "wasted our time." The reason is that the person praying is never alone. Above all, as well, God is at work.

HOW TO PRAY

We make distinctions concerning different types of prayer:

— meditation or the linking of ideas, for example: scenes from the gospels, texts from Mass.
— affective prayer which is a prayer where affection predominates; our prayer to Mary, for example, may be an example of affective prayer.
— simple prayer which is a presence where one is satisfied with a simple glance at a mystery, for example, the Trinity, the Incarnation, or the Eucharist.

One of the great principles of a life of prayer is faithfulness: "If you knew the gift of God" (Jn 4:10). We must pray for those we love, but above all, we must consider the divine mysteries, God within them. It is a simple, spontaneous conversation with Jesus which resolves itself in confident abandonment. We must aim at unlocking the door to the interior glance, at opening the interior eye. That will happen because Christ will be discovered to be a living and loved person.

For it is in prayer that the soul will realize that it is loved by the Lord.

Prayer is created so that our whole life is a prayer. This totality of prayer is why we get enlightenment, the strength to rise above our problems and fulfill our duties, the ability to forgive and know the divine will through it. It is through prayer that we perceive the direction for our life and what decisions we must make. In prayer, God's will becomes our nourishment.

But we don't only pray for ourselves; we pray to find God. We pray in order to find the love with which we want to love God and knowledge, which feeds love.

We must know how to find support from a gospel text which is very short and also when to leave it behind.

We must stand fast when prayer becomes difficult.

We must die, in effect, in prayer. A dry spell in certain specific cases may become a cause for enlightenment.

Prayer is a very pure exercise in the three theological virtues: faith, hope, and charity.

And then prayer will become apostolic and redemptive. Through prayer, we will perceive that God can be found in the smallest of our daily activities, that he is in the abbot, the brothers, and the guests.

It is by praying that we learn how to pray.

The more we pray, the more we want to pray.

The less we pray, the less we want to pray.

Prayer is like a field. In this field, there is a treasure—the union with God. We must dig for it without giving up.

It is a rendezvous of love.

He wants to hear us and speak to us. We just have to be aware of it through faith. It is a type of awakening.

In order to pray, we must follow Saint Benedict's advice: "First, with fervent prayer, beg of Him to finish the good work begun…" (RB, Prologue).

We must expect that God seems to withdraw, but this withdrawal is only to invite us to go further in our search for him. It is a divine process arranged so that we don't stop when we have reached just the small part of God that we only have begun to find. From God's viewpoint, it is a forward flight. He touches us, excites us, flees, and then comes back to incite us again. This heart-to-heart is never interrupted by God. If we interrupt it, he will come back to it through another path or road. We must be firm, accept the trial, leave what encumbers us behind, and prefer God to everything and in everything, imitate Jesus Christ, renew our desire and expectations of him through hope, finding our satisfaction in no one else. Thus, he will draw us out of ourselves, rip us from ourselves, and pour a greater degree of charity into our hearts.

The Lord hides himself so that the heart will seek him more ardently. The meeting is put off so that the person will find his own capacity for God and so that, one day, the believer will more fully find what he seeks. By appearing not to respond to our immediate desires, God intends to fulfill us even more. God neglects our request so that he can respond to his deeper intention.

The Lord calls the soul to a higher mountain, thus a greater love, and then, in this way, little by little, he lifts it and makes it grow. But in order to unite with it at the summit that he shows us now, it must descend into the valley (see RB, 7), descend as deeply as the summit is high.

THE GOAL OF PRAYER

Then, the goal of prayer gradually appears more clearly: "Anyone united to the Lord becomes one spirit with him" (1 Cor 6:17).

In prayer, truly "the Teacher is here and is calling for you" (Jn 11:28).

REFLECTION QUESTIONS

How often do I pray? How do I pray? Am I willing to try different methods of prayer? Have I considered centering prayer, praying the rosary, praying with a labyrinth, praying a litany, *lectio divina*, or others? Have I considered participating in various forms of nonliturgical communal prayers that might take place in my parish?

DAY FOURTEEN

Pure Prayer

FOCUS POINT

Pure prayer goes beyond biblical meditation and liturgical texts. Pure prayer is the monk's prayer, free from concepts, thoughts, and ideas, paying loving attention to God. There is a period of spiritual dryness that precedes pure prayer. This period is very difficult for the pray-er, as the pray-er journeys over uncharted ground, relying only on God in faith and trust.

Our prayer ought to be short and pure, unless by chance it is prolonged by the inspiration of Divine Grace (RB, 20).

PURITY OF HEART

Diligent reading of the Bible and its commentators, which are the works of the Fathers of the Church or the great masters of the spiritual life, will always be the setting of the monk's prayer. But reading is not prayer. It just gets us into the proper frame of mind. Cassian (360–435 A.D.), a journalist, who went to interview the monks of the East, came back to the West with the *Collations* (see RB, 42 and 73), which Saint Benedict knew and also which provided the goal of purity of heart to the monk. From this purity, pure prayer is born.

TO RECEIVE MANNA

After a certain amount of time, which seems rather short, the person who has the habit of meditating on biblical or liturgical texts will no longer be able to do so. He will then have to accept this "treatment"; it is the "night" which falls on the soul, the night which will progressively go on, that is to say, the soul traveling without enlightenment, in a complete absence of God, in an absolute void. The soul is invited to go beyond the sensory, to rest on faith, and to conduct itself completely through faith. It must learn to receive. To receive what? Manna. Therefore, it will no longer have its own thoughts, but passively pay loving attention to God. The soul must learn to beg, to live a naked faith, to remain in the interior desert in order to receive the manna—that is the monk's prayer.

Pure prayer signifies "purity," not only of evil or distracting thoughts, but in all idea, thought, and concept formations. To frequently seek, more and more in pure prayer, an intimate contact with the Absolute that the only partial total silence of the faculties give birth to beyond one's self, to enter into the depths, to allow oneself to fall all the way to the most intimate depth of our being where God lives and where his life radiates in us—that is the summit and the essence of prayer. It is a living mystery of presence. We must go all the way to the sacrifice of our distinctive and personal knowledge in order to leave all the room for God alone. The soul then offers a ground that is free and disengaged from all impediments. It is ready to passively receive the workings of God so that they may operate in the depths of the soul.

REFLECTION QUESTIONS

Am I willing to abandon all my notions of God, everything I "know" about the divine, so that I can make that all-important step into pure prayer? Do I desire a kind of prayer that is not driven by thoughts or concepts, but instead passively pays loving attention to God? Do I pray for the grace to leave everything I know (or think I know) about God in favor of actually sitting in his wordless presence?

DAY FIFTEEN

Summits

FOCUS POINT

Benedict lived the interior life; he lived a life of humility, and created in himself a place where God could dwell. Benedict allowed nothing to interfere with his love for God. With his Rule, Benedict was able to focus squarely on God, and gave to his community and to the world a means of centering one's life totally on God. Benedict realized that all the world is in God, and God is the most important part of our world. Anything else pales in comparison.

The light of contemplation enlarges the capacity of the soul. (D, 35)

THE WORLD IN GOD

Gregory tells us that Benedict realized the interior experience in its highest summits by means of a story and a conversation with Peter the Deacon: "When the time for rest had come, the venerable Benedict retired to the upper level of his tower, and the deacon Servandus to the lower level; the two rooms were connected by stairs and, in front of the tower, there was a larger room where the disciples of the two Fathers rested. While the disciples were still asleep, Benedict was still awake, in anticipation of the time for night prayers. Standing up in front of his window, he prayed to the all-powerful Lord, when suddenly, at this time of the night, he saw a light that chased the night away and shone with such a splendor that its light would make daylight seem pale. While he was looking at it, something extraordinary happened: later he told about it, the entire world was gathered before his eyes like a single ray of sunshine...Peter—How is it possible that the whole world could be seen by a single man?

"Gregory—Peter, remember what I say to you: for the one who sees the Creator, all of creation is seen in an abbreviated way. In as much as he caught a glimpse of the light of God, for him, all that is created becomes too narrow, for the light and contemplation broaden the capacity of the soul and through its repeated extension into God, it becomes higher than the world....

"When we say that the world was gathered before his eyes, it's not that the heavens and the earth are contracted, but that the soul of the believer is dilated...his spirit received an interior light which ravished his soul in God and showed him how restricted everything is that is not God" (D, 35).

Therefore, all other values, no matter how real, seem to be nothing in comparison to God. The Indians say that they are illusionary, maya. Swami Sivananda said: "The entire universe is in Brahman."[1] That is the All or nothing of Saint John of the Cross.

The world is in God, and the monk seeks God. And all the while we believed erroneously that the monk was cut off from the world, separated and fleeing from it. It is true that, in the beginning, it must have been like that, but, with the progression of his interior life, he finds the world again in God. Perhaps we could think of a certain parallel with the *ifrad* of Sufism (Hallaj) where the soul is isolated by God in order to participate in a mysterious divine solitude in which everything is given back but transformed and the prayer of the soul which is enamored by John of the Cross. Benedict, this man of prayer, this man of God who was, at the same time, both exacting and benevolent, possessed with a sense of the divine, a lover of transcendence, enamored with the absolute, impassioned with order, held contemplation for its supreme value. It is with the following words, written by Saint Benedict, that his reflections about how to live life ends:

> Whoever you are, if you wish to follow the path to God, make use of this little Rule for beginners. Thus, at length you will come to the heights of doctrine and virtue under God's guidance. Amen! (RB, 73).

The world in God. How did Benedict reach this summit? By cultivating interiority. It is this hidden value that gives meaning to the rest of the monk's life: liturgy, work, divine reading, study, the art of living together, a better life, a life in depth, and a life to the ultimate level. In fact, the one who interiorizes himself, the one who frees himself of himself will make the monk discover, in so much as the self is clothed by humility, a home for himself in God's self, a home that brings with it many homes and, "in this Other in ourselves, more of ourselves than ourselves," says Paul Claudel, he finds the world again. To realize that is true peace. It is through love that detachment from creation is accomplished for God and in God.

Benedict knew how to give birth to and maintain the desire for God that is the goal of monastic life. He knew how to create a school to serve God (see RB, Prologue), centered on "endless prayer" which is the soul of monastic life, by making his monk live for God, with God, and in God by giving him one single and unique task, that of seeking God. An expert on Benedictine monasticism, Dom Jean Leclercq, clearly saw the task of the monk in the Church: "Monks have this privilege of continuing to see. They know that they will not see the Lord: they will live in faith. And in the meantime, they will remain there. Their cross will be to love without seeing and, while always looking, to fix their eyes on nothing other than God, who is both invisible and present. Their witness before the world will be to show, by their very existence, the direction where we must look. It will be to hasten, through prayer and desire, the fulfillment of the kingdom of God."[2] They will be apostles through their monastic life—especially by the liturgy—persuaded that, as Jesus said, "Those who abide in me and I in them bear much fruit" (Jn 15:5).

JOHN PAUL II AND SAINT BENEDICT

In a speech given at Monte Cassino on the May 18, 1979, John Paul II declared:

> We could summarize that *the message of Saint Benedict is an invitation to interiority.* He lived alone with himself under the loving eyes of the Eternal Attentive One. Let us listen to the voice of Saint Benedict speaking about: interior solitude, contemplative silence, the victory over the agitation of the exterior world, this dwelling with one's self born from the dialogue between ourselves and God, which leads to the highest summit.

REFLECTION QUESTIONS

In what ways can I, as a humble creature, as a struggling prayer, reach the summits of love and unity with God that Benedict found? Might I consider a more disciplined prayer life? A more temperate and balanced approach to living? Might I consider praying to Benedict for perseverance in prayer and in living for God?

Notes

1. *Sivananda's Teachings (L'Enseignement de Sivananda)*, Albin Michel, Paris, 1958, p. 409.
2. *The Love of Knowledge and Desire for God (L'Amour des lettres at le désir de Dieu)*, Dom Jean Leclercq, Cerf, Paris, 1957, p. 59.

Bibliography

Benedict's Rule: A Translation & Commentary. Terrence G. Kardong. Liturgical Press, 1996.

Always We Begin Again: The Benedictine Way of Living. John McQuiston. Morehouse Publications, 1996.

A Life-Giving Way: A Commentary on the Rule of Saint Benedict. Esther De Waal. Liturgical Press, 1995.

The Life of Saint Benedict: Text & Commentary. Translated by Hilary Costello & Eon De-Bhaldraithe. St. Bedes Publications, 1993.

Reading Saint Benedict: Reflections on the Rule. Adalbert De Vogue (translated by Colette Friedlander). Cistercian Publications, 1994.

The Rule of Saint Benedict: A Doctrinal & Spiritual Commentary. Translated by John B. Hasbrouk. Cistercian Publications, 1983.

Seeking God: The Way of Saint Benedict. Liturgical Press, 1985.